Ablahad Lahdo

A Traitor among us

Semitica Viva

Herausgegeben von Otto Jastrow

Band 56

2017

Harrassowitz Verlag · Wiesbaden

Ablahad Lahdo

A Traitor among us
The Story of Father Yusuf Akbulut

A Text in the Ṭuroyo Dialect of ʿIwardo

2017
Harrassowitz Verlag · Wiesbaden

Bibliografische Information der Deutschen Nationalbibliothek
Die Deutsche Nationalbibliothek verzeichnet diese Publikation in der Deutschen Nationalbibliografie; detaillierte bibliografische Daten sind im Internet über http://dnb.dnb.de abrufbar.

Bibliographic information published by the Deutsche Nationalbibliothek
The Deutsche Nationalbibliothek lists this publication in the Deutsche Nationalbibliografie; detailed bibliographic data are available in the internet at http://dnb.dnb.de.

For further information about our publishing program consult our website http://www.harrassowitz-verlag.de

Printed on permanent/durable paper.
Printing and binding: Hubert & Co., Göttingen
Printed in Germany

ISSN 0931-2811
ISBN 978-3-447-10857-7

To father Yusuf Akbulut for his courageous stand

To the memory of the Syriac people who fell victim to the genocide one hundred years ago

Contents

Preface 9

Abbreviations and Symbols 11
Abbreviations 11
Symbols 11

Transcription signs 12
Consonants 12
Vowels 13
Vowels in borrowings 14
Diphthongs 14

Introduction 15
1.1. Aim and scope 16
1.2. The material 17
1.3. The informants 17
1.4. A short historical background 17
1.4.1. Diyarbakir 17
1.4.2. ʿIwardo 18
1.4.3. ʿIwardo today 21
1.4.4. Turkification 21
1.5. The legal case of father Yusuf Akbulut 22

2. Some linguistic remarks 26
2.1. On phonology 26
2.1.1. Assimilation 26
2.2. On morphology 26
2.2.1. The definite article 26
2.2.2. The prefix *ko-* 27
2.2.3. Elicited data 27
2.2.4. Verb paradigms 27
2.2.4 Transcription and translation 35

3. Text 1 36

4. Translation text 1 45

5. Text 2 55

6. Translation text 2 67

Idioms 79

Glossary 81

References 107

Preface

In November 2004, during a visit to Tur Abdin, I visited the Syriac Orthodox Church of St. Mary's in Diyarbakir. Some years earlier I had closely followed the events taking place at this very site, in this same city. What was eye-catching for me, when entering the gate to the church's courtyard, was that the main street was narrow and the quarter was crowded. The church was totally surrounded by houses that were of the same height or higher, a fact that made me wonder how such a small community of few Syriac families could live entirely surrounded by Kurds. My apprehension was unfortunately confirmed later on in the evening. While sitting in the church's courtyard drinking tea, a thump made me almost jump up from my chair. I looked around and noticed that I was the only one that reacted, as if the others did not hear the noise. I asked father Yusuf Akbulut if he heard anything and he answered that he heard and that this was nothing to worry about. It was probably just some people passing the gate and either kicked it or tossed a stone at it. This has become part of our daily life here, the priest explained miserably. This incident kept me awake all that night wondering how a normal everday life looked like for these underprivileged people in this part of the world. I further wondered: how many people out there know about this?

On October 5, 2000, father Akbulut was apprehended and questioned by police in Diyarbakir for 18 hours. The day before, a report in the daily newspaper *Hurriyet* had accused him of making statements that supported labeling the death of Armenians during World War I as genocide. Syrian Orthodox Christians also experienced genocide, not only the Armenians, the priest had added.

Father Akbulut was put on trial, and three hearings later he was proclaimed not guilty. Almost four years later, he and his family were still suffering from harassment. When I next interviewed father Akbulut, in April 2014, it was obvious that life was still very unpleasant for the priest and for his family.

Thus, one hundred years after the genocide that nearly erased all Christians in general and the Syrian Orthodox community in particular, the descendants of the few that survived the slaughter are still facing harassment in today's Turkey, a Turkey that has otherwise made enormous efforts to be part of the European community.

With this book I would like to honor all the Syriac people all over the world in general and those who still live in Turkey and Tur Abdin in particular. Father Yusuf Akbulut was called a traitor in the Turkish media but for the Syriac people he is a hero because at risk for his own and his families' lives he dared tell the truth. I owe father Akbulut my deepest gratitude for being open concerning what he went through and for granting me these interviews which comprise the core this book.

Ablahad Lahdo

Uppsala March 2017

Abbreviations and Symbols

Abbreviations

Ara. — Arabic
c. — communis
C — consonant
e.g. — exempli gratia (for example)
Eng. — English
f. — Feminine
i.e. — id est (that is)
Kur. — Kurdish
m. — Masculine
lit. — Literally
pl. — Plural
sg. — Singular
s.o. — Someone
s.th. — Something
Syr. — Syriac (Classical Syriac)
Tur. — Turkish

Symbols

1 — first person
2 — second person
3 — third person
< — developed or originates from (not necessarily diachronic)
> — developed to
* — a form not attested
.., — an unfinished word
... — an unfinished sentence
() — in translations, meaning that a word or an expression is added for the sake of clarification
→ — see under

Transcription signs

Consonants

Sign	Pronunciation	Description	As in Eng.
ʾ	[ʔ]	voiceless glottal plosive	*uh oh*
ʿ	[ʕ]	voiced laryngeal fricative	
b	[b]	voiced bilabial plosive	*ball*
č	[tʃ]	voiceless palato-alveolar affricate	*chair*
d	[d]	voiced dental plosive	*do*
ḏ	[ð]	voiced interdental fricative	*the*
ḍ	[dˤ]	voiced velarized dental plosive	*dawn*
ḏ̣	[ðˤ]	voiced velarized fricative	*velarized ḏ*
f	[f]	voiceless labio-dental fricative	*fear*
g	[g]	voiced velar plosive	*God*
ġ	[ɣ]	voiced velar fricative	
ǧ	[dʒ]	voiced palato-alveolar affricate	*general*
h	[h]	voiceless glottal fricative	*happy*
ḥ	[ħ]	voiceless laryngeal fricative	
k	[k]	voiceless velar plosive	*cat*
l	[l]	voiced dental lateral	*live*
m	[m]	voiced velarized bilabial nasal	*meat*
n	[n]	voiced velarized dental nasal	*near*
p	[p]	voiceless bilabial plosive	*pull*
q	[q]	voiceless uvular plosive	
r	[r]	voiced velarized dental trill	*red*
s	[s]	voiceless dental sibilant	*sun*
ṣ	[sˤ]	voiceless velarized dental	*sod*

		sibilant	
š	[ʃ]	voiceless palato-alveolar sibilant	*she*
t	[t]	voiceless dental plosive	*ten*
ṭ	[ɫ]	voiceless velarized dental plosive	*toddy*
ṯ	[θ]	voiceless interdentals fricative	*thanks*
v	[v]	voiced velarized labio-dental	*very*
w	[w]	voiced labio-velar	*will*
x	[x]	voiceless velar fricative	
y	[j]	voiced palatal	*yes*
z	[z]	voiced dental sibilant	*zoo*
ẓ	[ɀ]	voiced velarized dental sibilant	
ž	[ʒ]	palate-alveolar sibilant	*television*

Consonants with a dot under, e.g.: *ḍ, ṣ, ḷ, ṇ, ṭ, ẓ* etc. are verlarized in comparison with their counterpart. *č, ğ,* and *ž* have come into Turoyo from Turkish, Kurdish and Arabic. Some phonemes have no counterparts in English and therefore are not exemplified.

Vowels

Sign	Pronunciation	Description
i	[ɪ]	short front unrounded
e	[e]	front unrounded
a	[a]	short front-to-back unrounded
ə	[ə]	short middle unrouded
u	[ʊ]	short back rounded
o	[o]	short back rounded
ī	[i:]	long front unrounded
ē	[e:]	long front unrounded
ā	[a:]	long front-to-back unrounded

ū	[u:]	long back rounded
ō	[o:]	long back rounded

All unmarked vowels in an open syllable are to be read as long.
Long vowels in close syllables are marked with macron (¯), e.g.: *u=mŭdūr* "director"; *kŭltūr* "culture"; *kīt* "there is"; *sūğ* "guilt, fault, blame".

Short vowels in an open syllable are marked with a breve (˘), e.g.: *ġălăbe* "much, a lot"; *u=ğăsădano* "this body"; *tahlŭkat* "danger"; *inṣān ḥaqlări* "human rights".

Vowels in borrowings

Sign	Pronunciation	Description
ö	[œ]	short front rounded
ü	[y]	short front rounded

E.g.: *Hürriyet* "a daily newspaper"; *güwanlək* "security"; *örnak* "example".

Diphthongs

Sign	Pronunciation	Description
ay	[aɪ]	my
aw	[aʊ]	how

The diphthongs *ăw* and *ăy* are retained in Turoyo, e.g.: *băyto* "home, hous"; *măwto* "death". In the texts below the breve over the diphthong is not written.

1. Introduction

Turoyo (Ṭūrōyo, Ṣūrayt) is a Neo-Aramaic dialect or a dialect group with its original homeland in Tur Abdin, in today's Southeast Turkey. Because of the long-lasting persecutions of Christians during the Ottoman Empire and that culminated in massive deportations and massacres in 1915, most of the villages of Tur Abdin, including their district city Midyat, are today nearly empty of their Turoyo speakers. Some Turoyo dialects have already vanished others have just a few speakers left. In the diaspora, where different dialects come together, differences between dialects are predestined to disappear. According to Jastrow, the survival of Turoyo is closely tied up with the fate of the original homeland, Tur Abdin.[1] In 1970 there were approximately 20 000 Turoyo speakers in Tur Abdin and today only a few thousand.[2] If Turoyo would vanish totally, we would lose one of the few languages in the world that have a language continuum of more than two thousand years!

While the extinct dialects of Aramaic have attracted, and continue to attract a great deal scholarly attention, the living varieties had sadly a history of being neglected. The interest in Neo-Aramaic initiated in the mid-nineteenth century in some articles and even a few monographs, e.g. T. Nöldeke's *Grammatik der neusyrischen Sprachen am Urmia-see und in Kurdistan*, A. J. Maclean's *Grammar* and *Dictionary of the Dialects of Vernacular Syriac,* and A. Siegel's *Laut- und Formenlehre des neuaramäischen Dialekts des Ṭûr ʿAbdîn.* G. Bergsträsser's *Introduction to the Semitic Languages* deals with Neo-Aramaic and thereby encourages Semitists to resist the temptation to focus on older periods of the Semitic languages in their comparative endeavours.

The last five to six decades have seen a great deal of activity in recording, documenting, and analysing Neo-Aramaic dialects. Several volumes have been published in series such as Handbuch der Orientalistik, Studies in Semitic Languages and Linguistics and especially Semitica Viva. Neo-Aramaic dialects are divided into four different groups:

1 Jastrow 1987, 9.

2 Jastrow 1987, 7 and Tezel 2011, preface.

1. Western Neo-Aramaic, i.e. the dialect of Maʿlula, Baxʿa and Ǧubb ʿadin in the Qalamun mountains in Syria
2. Western or Western side of Eastern Neo-Aramaic, i.e. Turoyo and Mlaḥsô
3. Eastern Aramaic, i.e. Modern or Neo-Mandaic
4. North-eastern Neo-Aramaic (NENA)

In his monumental five-volume work on Turoyo, *Ṭūrōyo: die Volkssprache der syrischen Christen des Ṭūr ʿAbdīn* (1967-1990), Helmut Ritter gathered material from different Turoyo speakers representing different villages of Tur Abdin. It won't be an exaggeration to assert that Ritter, with his grammar, glossary and text volumes, laid the foundation for modern studies of these Neo-Aramaic vernaculars. The dialect of Midən, the largest Turoyo speaking village in the Tur Abdin, has received outstanding descriptions in Otto Jastrow's *Laut- und Formenlehre des neuaramäischen Dialekts von Mīdin im Ṭūr ʿAbdin*. This study was first published in 1967 and then in 1993 in Semitica Viva 9. The textbook *Lehrbuch der Ṭuroyo-Sprache* was published in 1992. In 1968, while conducting field-work gathering data from the westernmost of the so called *qəltu*-dialects' regions, in the district of Diyarbakir, Jastrow discovered a previously unknown Neo-Aramaic language, namely Mlaḥsô. The Christians of Mlaḥsô were massacred in 1915 and the few survivors that Jastrow met were among the last to speak this language. They are now all dead, which in turn means that also the language of Mlaḥsô is extinct. Jastrow presented his discovery in an article in *Journal of Semitic Studies* in 1985. In 1994 Jastrow published *Der neuaramäische Dialekt von Mlaḥsô* (Semitica Viva 14). This publication consists of a grammatical outline, texts and a glossary. The book also includes comparative notes. *Der Turoyo-Dialekt von Midyat* is one of the works in progress that Jastrow has on his desk at the moment.

1.1. Aim and scope

As mentioned above, many Neo-Aramaic dialects are in danger of extinction and there is an urgent need for documenting as many as possible before it is too late. Text materials from the different dialects of the villages of Tur Abdin are rare, except for Midən. By publishing genuine Turoyo material from the village of ʿIwardo I aim to contribute to the study of these endangered Neo-Aramaic dialects.

1.2. The material

The first part of the material below, i.e. text 1, was tape-recorded in St. Mary's Church in Diyarbakir in November 2004. In this text, father Akbulut narrates in his own words and in detail what happened from the day the journalists of *Hurriyet* approached him in the church's courtyard until he was found not guilty, six months later, after the third hearing. Text 2 was recorded in April 2014. In this text, the priest recounts the mistreatment he and his family are suffering from on an everyday basis because of the publicity. The material in the verb paradigms was tape-recorded in Sweden.

1.3. The informants

The main informant of the texts below is father Yusuf Akbulut, who was 40 years old in 2004 when the first interview with him was made. For the sake of having some complete verb paradigms, and for comparison with forms attested in the material, some elicited data was recorded from two other informants living in Sweden. These informants are a 83 year-old man who was born in ʿIwardo but left it when he was ten years old and a 52 year-old man who was born in Qamishli, Syria, of parents originating from ʿIwardo. Some forms that are attested in the material and that in some way differ from the Turoyo dialect of Midən are noted.

1.4. A short historical background

1.4.1. Diyarbakir

Diyarbakir is a large city on a basalt plateau by the Tigris with mainly Kurdish inhabitants. The importance which was attached to this city can be measured by the length and breadth of the wall which stretches 5.5 km (6 km in some sources) around the city. Vital to the Roman defense of Mesopotamia against the Persian Empire, Diyarbakir was conquered by the Arabs in 639, by the Seljuks in 1085, and by Sultan Selim I in 1515.[3]

Amida in Ancient Greek refers to today's Diyarbakir. Amid, or Omid, which is the Syriac name, is inscribed on the sheath of a sword from the Assyrian period, and the same name was used in other contemporary Syriac and Arabic works. The Romans and Byzantines called the city Amida. Among the Artukid and Akkoyunlu it was known as Black Amid, Kara Amid in

3 Hollerweger 1999, 335-337.

Turkish, because of the dark color of its walls, while in the Zafername, or eulogies in praise of military victories, it is called the Black Fortress, Kara Kale, in Turkish. In the Book of Dede Korkut and some other Turkish works it appears as Kara Hamid,[4] as a step towards Turkification.

Following the Arab conquests in the seventh century, the Arab Bakr tribe occupied this region, which became known as the Diyar Bakr "landholdings of the Bakr tribe". In 1937, Atatürk visited Diyarbekir and, after expressing uncertainty on the exact etymology of the city, ordered that it be renamed "Diyarbakır", which means "land of copper" in Turkish, given the abundant resources of copper around the city.

Already in the fourth century Omid was an episcopal see. In the Middle Ages the Syrian Orthodox Patriarch resided here. Today there are only a few Christian families left in the city. The present Church of St. Mary's[5] is all that remains of a great cathedral from perhaps the sixth century. The nave of that cathedral broadened into a round church towards the west. On either side of the apse one can still admire the Corinthian capitals with the garlands typical of this area and the finely sculpted remains of the ancient sanctuary arch. These remains speak expressively of the size and beauty of the original building.[6]

Northwards of the apse, one enters another church with three altars and the tomb of Jacob Serugh (451-521), a learned bishop who, like St. Ephraim in the 4th century, taught through the medium of poetry set to music. Next to the church one can see the patriarchal residence of the 19th century.

1.4.2. ʿIwardo

ʿIwardo (Inwardo, Aynwardo and Turkish Gülgöze) is built on a hill some two hours walk from Midyat. The name of the village means “The source of the rose”. When approaching ʿIwardo, for example from Midyat, one crosses a long and broad valley at the end of which a fortress-like construction appears.[7] The colossal building of the church of Mor Hushabo stands on the peak of the hill and it is surrounded by strong walls and defensible towers, in which the bullets from the time of the siege can been seen still today. It is probable that the location of ʿIwardo and the way it was constructed, i.e. as a stronghold, were some of the reasons why many Christians from the

4 Greatrex and Lieu 2002, 82–97.

5 In some literature, for example Hollerweger, the term “Mother of God” is used. The Turkish name is Meryemana kilisesi. Cf. Syr. **yoldāṯ aḷoho* “God bearer”.

6 Hollerweger 1999, 334-337.

7 Hollerweger 1999, 118-119.

neighbouring villages and from Midyat sought their protection in it during the massacres of 1915.

Among the Syriac people, still today one can hear about the brave people of ʿIwardo. As a matter of fact, ʿIwardo did what the majority of the villages of Tur Abdin could not do, namely defend itself against the attacking Turks and Kurds. According to Armale, ʿIwardo and Azakh are the only two villages in Mesopotamia that offered resistance and fought effectively against the Turks.[8] The village played, as a consequence, an important role during these massacres, not only because the villagers of ʿIwardo protected themselves and their village, but also because they helped other Christians[9] flee deportation convoys and slaughter. They also send detachment of combatants to rescue Christian hostages held in Kurdish villages.[10]

At the time of the massacres, 200 Syriac Orthodox families lived in ʿIwardo and no Muslims. By the summer of 1915, between 6000 and 7000 Syriac Christians from Bote, Habses, Kafarbe, Kafro, Midyat and Zaz took their refuge in the village. The refugees reported all the horrifying ordeals that their close ones had suffered and the fate that their villages had met. Hearing all this, Mas'ud Mzizakhi, a local leader in ʿIwardo, assembled in a relatively short time some 700 men. At night they would dress in black and go out to rescue people who had survived execution squads or escaped from deportation convoys.[11]

---

8 Armale 2005, 383.

9 In this context, Christians mean speakers of Neo-Aramaic, Turoyo, who belong to the Syriac Orthodox Church. But in general the term Christians, during these massacres, meant Turoyo speakers, speakers of east Neo-Aramaic, Armenians and Greeks.

10 In page 234 Gaunt writes the following about the Syriacs of Kfarze: When the news of the massacres arrived, the Christian villagers held a council. Some wanted to arm themselves, but the majority put their hopes in the promises of the government authorities that they would be safe. The Kurds, however, prepared to massacre their neighbors, and news of this was leaked to the Christians. The villagers sent word to ʿAyn-Wardo asking for help. On the night that the Kurds set for the attack, well-armed men from ʿAyn-Wardo arrived and helped the Christians to flee. The Kurds observed this flight, and there was hard fighting. Many survived and reached ʿAyn-Wardo, while others took refuge in the neighboring Muslim villages of Dermuske and Kafsange, where they were held hostage. The Syriacs sent out a detachment of 300 men to free the hostages held in Dermuske. They attacked the village and freed their relatives and neighbors and captured the sister of the Kurdish chieftain, Abdulramhman in order to exchange her for the other Christians. But 86 Syriac hostages were still in Kurdish hands in Kafsange, and these were marched out of the village to be killed. At that moment, Abdulrahman sent a message not to harm the hostages. Instead, an exchange of the hostages for his sister was agreed upon. The villagers remained in ʿAyn -Wardo throughout the war.

11 Gaunt 2006, 202.

When the news about the men of ʿIwardo reached the provincial governor of Midyat, he prepared for a large-scale assault against the village. He gathered a 13 000 man strong army, mostly Kurdish tribes from the Midyat and Mardin areas, supplied it with weapons, ammunition and food from the government warehouses and sent it to destroy ʿIwardo. On an unspecified Friday in the middle of July the army surrounded ʿIwardo and heavy fighting began. The outnumbered and outgunned Syriacs launched counterattacks under the cover of darkness, and although they suffered many casualties, the Turkish and Kurdish losses were much greater. The full-scale war continued for about 10 days and the Turkish commandant ordered a final large-scale charge for Sunday morning when the church bells started to ring. This attack was only partially successful. Another massive attack was made on Tuesday but this one failed completely; the Turks lost 50 men, including a high-ranking officer. The result of this caused confusion and shock in the aggressor's lines.[12]

The siege of ʿIwardo lasted for 52 days, according to Armale.[13] The aggressors found themselves forced to negotiate with the Syriacs of ʿIwardo. They sent different mediators, all of whom were refused by the Syriacs. At last the Syriacs asked for one specific mediator, Shaykh Fathulla from ʿAyn Kif, a Muhallemi Kurd. On his arrival, the Syriacs placed themselves under his protection. Shaykh Fathulla persuaded the Turks to order the Kurds to leave and guarantee the Syriacs free passage. Only after the aggressors were ordered to leave, was Shayk Fathulla able to collect the Syriacs' weapons. Despite the guarantee of amnesty, most of the Syriacs remained in the village and did not dare return to their original villages. The few ones who dared were shot on their way back, for example to ʿArnas, Ahlah and Mizizah.[14] Hanna Savaro, a 73-year-old man in 2010 was interviewed by Jan Beṯ Sawoce recounts what he heard from his father:

bəṯər məd-qayimo (i=ʿaskar), hedi an=nošayḏan, kəḏʿat u=ʕlām kfoyəš tloṯo yarḥe bu=.., lawġəl, howe əysīr, malḥo lə=kfoyəš, qamḥo lə=kfoyəš, qayse lə=kfoyəš, he bizi an=nošayḏan, kŭl=ḥa d-azzé b-dŭkṯo. u=ḥa yawmo azzé ʿaṣro, ḥamšaḥṣar, čaḥṣar gawre, azzən li=Xalbube d-moṭənne qayse. disa u=ʿammo d-babi d-kənno b-əšme baynaṯṯe-wa. tamo aṯən as=saliyye maḥətte i=kawmo, tamo qṭəlle ač=čaḥṣar. ḥatta ʿammi šməṭṭe ṣawʿoṯe w i=tfəgayḏe bu=zor məfqəlle m-iḏe. qṭile ḥa-sti u səmle ḥa-sti brindar.[15] *w aṯən šməṭṭe i=tfəng.., ṣawʿoṯe w mədde*

12 Gaunt 2006, 204 and Armale 2005, 384.

13 Armale 2005, 387.

14 Gaunt 2006, 204-205.

15 Cf. Kur. *brîndar* or *birîndar* "wounded, injured".

li=tfəngayḏe. w ḥatta hŭl ʿayne, əmmi məfqənne məblənne la=sohraniyye, me-Slemane Nəʿmat, sohraniyye. … qṭəlle čaḥṣaṟ gawre b-ḥa yawmo. mṭanne maḥtənne kŭlle bi=dərto d-Mar Ḥušabo.

"After that (the soldiers) had left, well our people, as you know, when a man is kept in the, inside, he becomes (like) a prisoner, there won't be any salt left, there won't be any flour left, there won't be any firewood left, so our people went out, each one went somewhere. One day ten, fifteen, nineteen men went to Xalbube to gather firewood. Again, my father's uncle, the one I am named after was among them. There, where they put the pile (of the firewood) the Saliyyes came and killed all of them. They even chopped my uncle's fingers and took his rifle; they had difficulties releasing it from his hands. He even killed one of them and injured one. So they came and took his rifl.., chopped his fingers and took his rifle and they went so far that even his eyes, it is said that they put them out and took them to Sohraniyye. … They killed nineteen men in one single day. They brought them and put them in the courtyard of St. Hushabo."

1.4.3. ʿIwardo today

As mentioned above, at the time of the massacres some 200 Syriac Orthodox families lived in ʿIwardo and no Muslims. Today there are less than ten Syriac families left in the village. There is no priest in the famous church of St. Hushabo any longer. On occasions such as funerals or baptisms a priest from Midyat comes and performs the service and then leaves. This is very sad, my informant adds.

More than twenty Kurdish families live in ʿIwardo today, and the number of Kurds is increasing. My oldest informant, who visited his home village four years ago, says that he has heard that Kurds have now built a mosque in the village, but this is not totally sure. If so is the case, I believe that the mosque is just symbolic for the Kurds while for the Christians it is a clear signal, i.e. they will have to listen to the muezzin, the Muslims call for prayer 5 times a day, while no church bells are ringing any longer, he continues. Fewer than ten families left, mostly old people, a delapidated church with no priest, a strong presence of Kurds, well this is our ʿIwardo today, he concludes.

1.4.4. Turkification

After the foundation of the republic of Turkey in the early 1920s, a process of "Turkification" started. Two elements in this process are of paticular interest in this connection and should be mentioned:

1. According to the Surname Act, *Soyadı kanunu*, of 28 June 1934, all people living in Turkey must have surnames.[16]

2. All names of cities, towns and villages must be derived from Turkish words. However, this principle was not enshrined in law but followed recommendations from officials such as the local government commissioner, the local municipal council, etc.

Henceforth, no matter what ethnic background a Turkish citizen had, he or she must have a Turkish surname. All the Syrian Orthodox people born and registered in Turkey have Turkish surnames, which makes it hard to distinguish them from other Turks. Akbulut "white cloud" is hence a Turkish surname that father Akbulut must have notwithstanding the knowledge that the Turks, together with the Kurds, massacred his ancestors and his people.

1.5. The legal case of father Yusuf Akbulut

On October 5, 2000, father Yusuf Akbulut, the parish priest of St. Mary's Church in Diyarbakir, was detained and questioned by police in Diyarbakir for 18 hours. The day before, a sensationalized report in the mass-circulation daily *Hurriyet* had accused father Akbulut of making statements that supported a pending resolution in the US House of Representatives calling on President Bill Clinton to officially label the death of Armenians during World War I as genocide.

According to church sources, father Akbulut, a native of the village ʿIwardo in Tur Abdin, was "baited" with questions about the genocide issue while talking with friends at a local teahouse. The priest was supposedly not aware that any of his questioners were journalists.[17]

16 Aktar 2009, 47 (note 32); Lewis 2000, 289; Ballı 1991, 65 and Arnold 2000, 357. People from these regions related that the authorities sent officials to the villages with a list of Turkish names and every family had to choose one. The ones who did not choose were given a family name that the officials chose for them.

17 Compass Direct, December 15, 2000 by Barbara G. Baker. Barbara G. Baker followed the issue of father Akbulut closely and wrote several articles about it. Upon request, she sent me all that she had written.

Father Akbulut, 36 years at the time, is married and has five children. He has been serving as the parish priest for this small Syrian Orthodox community in Diyarbakir from early 1990's.

Father Akbulut was charged under Article 312 of the Turkish Penal Code, which criminalizes provoking "religious or ethnic enmity". If convicted, the priest could have been imprisoned from one up to three years. Father Akbulut was put on trial December 21, 2000 before Diyarbakir's Second State Security Court, where he declared under oath that he had refused to be interviewed by the journalists, agreeing only to chat with them "off the record". Father Akbulut told the judge that he was not aware that the reporter had taped his comments with a video camera as they talked under a tree in the courtyard of St. Mary's Syrian Orthodox Church, where he still lives with his family. In Father Akbulut's comments, which he did not retract, he had referred to "Syrian Orthodox Christians who also experienced genocide, not only the Armenians".

The Turkish journalists who testified for the prosecution claimed in court that they had interviewed father Akbulut in a typical question-answer format and that he knew they planned to publish his comments. However, they differed among themselves as to whether he said these were his personal views or was quoting others' opinions. Father Akbulut's attorney emphasized that his client had been the target of a deliberate plot and requested the court to acquit his client without further wrongful injury. Furthermore, the lawyer continued, the real perpetrators in this case should be the journalists. The attorney told the judge declaring that it was they who had violated press ethics and also deliberately incited ethno-religious enmity. The attorney filed a court exhibit of an interview published by *Radikal* newspaper on November 9, 2000, featuring comments from Professor Halil Berktay, a historian from Sabanci University specializing in 19th and 20th century Turkish history. "His comments were much stronger than those made by my client", the lawyer pointed out, "but no case has been opened against him or his newspaper".[18] At the close of the hearing, the presiding judge ordered a copy of father Akbulut's comments, recorded on video by *Hurriyet* reporter and later aired on TV Channel D, to be submitted to the court. The footage would be examined at the next hearing, set for February 22, 2001.

In the courtroom, some 60 visitors crowded for the hour-long hearing, including a dozen foreigners and scores of Turkish journalists and cameramen. The diplomatic missions of Germany, the Netherlands, the

18 Compass Direct, January 19, 2001 by Barbara G. Baker.

United States and Sweden all sent observers. Other representatives include members of the European, Swedish and German parliaments, a political officer from the European Union, and two German representatives of Sign of Hope, a Christian human rights advocacy group.

According to one Swedish Member of Parliament, 65 members of the Swedish Parliament had signed a letter of inquiry about father Akbulut's case that was forwarded to the Turkish government just before the trial.

As it is mentioned in text 1 below, father Akbulut was not mistreated physically during his lengthy interrogation in early October 2000. However, he found it particularly insulting when he was asked why he still insisted on speaking Syriac (Neo-Aramaic, Turoyo) with his family, instead of Turkish. Father Akbulut and the majority Syrian Orthodox Christians pride themselves in keeping alive a Neo-Aramaic dialect close to that spoken by Jesus in the first century. It is the language still used in family life today.

Gabriele Yonan, author of "The Assyrian Genocide: An Unforgettable Holocaust" and an observer who came from Berlin for the trial, said she was puzzled that the Turkish state could claim the priest's comments constituted a crime at the same time granting her book publishing rights in Turkish. "How is it possible that one can buy such a book here freely, but on the other hand, there is this court case against father Akbulut, who said briefly exactly what is printed in my 400 pages?"

After the court hearing, the Chief Prosecutor told some of the foreign observers who met him in his office that he was "optimistic on the outcome" of the trial. "It is our desire that diplomats have correct information, and not judge cases here ignorantly. We cannot accept any attempt to depreciate Turkey".[19]

In the third and final hearing on the case on April 5, 2001, the state prosecutor declared that analysis of the video recording of the priest's comments indicated that this case was "an issue of freedom of thought". Although father Akbulut had in fact made the statements quoted in the Turkish press, the prosecutor observed, these privately stated opinions did not constitute a public attempt to provoke hatred. Accordingly, with no proof found to substantiate the indictment, the prosecutor asked the court to acquit the defendant. The judicial bench required less than five minutes of consultation before announcing their verdict. Many observers in the

---

19 Ibid.

courtroom broke into applause when the presiding judge announced the acquittal.

The defense attorney spoke to Compass Direct by telephone from Diyarbakir and said “this is a very positive and important decision for Turkey. I believe it can only help our relations with Europe, to emphasize the direction we are heading in to encourage and strengthen freedom of thought among all our citizens”.[20]

Although a number of international observers and local press had attended the previous hearings on December 21, 2000 and February 22, 2001, the courtroom was even more crowded during the April 5, 2001 hearing. There was a large Swedish delegation and two members of the German Parliament, along with other diplomatic representatives, and lots of press people.[21]

Following father Akbulut’s case, some questions come to one’s mind, for example: What would have happened if the international community had not shown interest in father Akbulut’s process? Would the outcome of the first hearing have been the same? What happens to “normal” people who are defendants against similar allegations?

---

20 Compass Direct, April 20, 2001 by Barbara G. Baker.
21 Ibid.

2. Some linguistic remarks

2.1. On phonology

2.1.1. Assimilation

In verb conjugation the following assimilation appears:

rn > *ṇṇ*, e.g.: *omaṇṇo* “I said” < *omarno*
rl > *ḷḷ*, e.g.: *ḥəḷḷi* “I looked” < *ḥərli*
rC > *ṛṛ*, e.g.: *məṛṛe* “they said” < **mərlən*

tn> *nn*, e.g.: *lanna* “we are not” < *latna*
ln > *nn*, e.g.: *komaqbanno* “I accept” < *komaqbalno*
nl > *ll*, e.g.: *komoḥkəlli* “the tell me” < **komaḥkənli*

Voiced consonants may shift to voiceless in contact position before a voiceless consonant, i.e. partial regressive assimilation, e.g.: *haṯe yḏəḥto-yo* “this is known”, cf. *odəʿ* - *adəʿ* “he knows”. Also the relative pronoun *d-* is affected by regressive assimilation, e.g.: *u=mede t-səmme* ... “what they have done ...”; *kito hənn t-ṣayimiwa* “there are some who fasted”. This may be due to Turkish influence.[22]

2.2. On morphology

2.2.1. The definite article

The definite article is *u=* for masculine, *i=* for feminine and *a=* for plural, e.g.: *u=yawmo* “the day”; *i=šato* “the year”; *a=ʿlayme* “the young men”. But when a noun in plural begins with only one consonant, the first consonant is doubled, e.g.: *buġre* > *ab=buġre* “the bullets”; *garme* > *ag=garme* “the bones”; *noše* > *an=noše* “the people”, *səryoye* > *as=səryoye* “the Syriac people”. Nouns that begin with a vowel have the definite article *ann=*, e.g.: *alfowat* > *ann=alfowat* “the thousands”; *əšmone* > *ann=əšmone* “the names”; *arʿoṯe* > *ann=arʿoṯe* “the lands”. The same applies for foreign names and loan-words that begin with a vowel, e.g.: *armənoye* > *ann=armənoye* “the Armenians”.

22 Lahdo 2009, 45-46.

2.2.2. The prefix *ko-*

The prefix *ko-* precedes a verb to indicate actual present, e.g.: *domәx - damәx - kodomәx* "he sleeps, is asleep"; *howe - hawi – kowe* "it happens"; *maḥke - maḥkele – komaḥke* "he tells".

2.2.3. Elicited data

Some of the verbs that are common in Turoyo and that occur frequently in the texts below are taken into the glossary where also other attested forms of the same verb are presented. Nevertheless, since the informant, i.e. father Akbulut, is just one speaker of this Turoyo dialect (in this aspect), another ʿiwarnoyo was therefore consulted. The reason for this was, on the one hand to see if these two informants have the exact same pronunciation of the verbs and on the other hand to have complete paradigms for the mentioned verbs.[23] In some instances, a comparison is made with the Turoyo dialect of Midәn.

2.2.4. Verb paradigms

The verb *domәx – damәx (kodomәx)*

	sg.	pl.		
3.m.	*damәx*	*Damixi*	*kodomәx*	*kodәmxi*
3.f.	*damixo*		*kodәmxo*	
2.m.	*damixat*	*Damixutu*	*kodәmxat*	*kodәmxutu*
2.f.	*damixat*		*kodәmxat*	
1.m.	*damәxno*	*Damixina*	*kodomaxno*	*kodәmxina*
1.f.	*damixono*		*kodәmxono*	

Midәn 2.m.sg. *damixәt.*[24]

The verb *fotәḥ – ftәḥle (kofotәḥ)*

	sg.	pl.		
3.m.	*ftәḥle*	*ftәḥḥe*	*kofotәḥ*	*kofәtḥi*
3.f.	*ftәḥla*		*kofәtḥo*	

23 It is important to keep in mind that elicited data are often obtained by addressing questions to an informant. The informant then answers how a word is pronounced in this dialect. The word is then out of its context, which may often lead to a slightly different pronunciation, compared to when a word is a part of a sentence.

24 Cf. Jastrow 2002, 122.

2.m.	*ftəḥlox*	*ftəḥxu*	*kofətḥat*	*kofətḥutu*
2.f.	*ftəḥlax*		*kofətḥat*	
1.m.	*ftəḥli*	*ftəḥlan*	*kofotaḥno*	*kofətḥina*
1.f.	*ftəḥli*		*kofətḥono*	

The verb *foyəš - fayəš (kofoyəš)*

	sg.	pl.		
3.m.	*fayəš*	*fayiši*	*kofoyəš*	*kofayši*
3.f.	*fayišo*		*kofayšo*	
2.m.	*fayišat*	*fayišutu*	*kofayšat*	*kofayšutu*
2.f.	*fayišat*		*kofayšat*	
1.m.	*fayəšno*	*fayišina*	*kofoyašno*	*kofayšina*
1.f.	*fayšono*		*kofayšono*	

The verb *howe – hawi (kowe)*

	sg.	pl.		
3.m.	*hawi*	*hawən*	*kowe*	*kowən*
3.f.	*hawyo*		*kuyo*	
2.m.	*hawat*	*hawutu*	*kowat*	*kowutu*
2.f.	*hawat*		*kowat*	
1.m.	*hawino*	*hawina*	*koweno*	*kowino*
1.f.	*hawyono*		*kuyono*	

Midən 2.m.sg. *howət;* 2.f.sg. *huyat.*[25]

The verb *ḥoyər – ḥəṛle* and *ḥəḷḷe (koḥoyər)*

	sg.	pl.		
3.m.	*ḥəṛle*	*ḥəṛṛe*	*koḥoyəṛ*	*koḥayṛi*
3.f.	*ḥəṛla*		*koḥayṛo*	
2.m.	*ḥəṛlox*	*ḥəṛxu*	*koḥayṛat*	*koḥayṛutu*
2.f.	*ḥəṛlax*		*koḥayṛat*	

25 Cf. Jastrow 2002, 41.

1.m.	*ḥəṛli*	*ḥəṛlan*	*koḥoyaṛno*	*koḥayṛina*
1.f.			*koḥayṛono*	

The expected assimilation of *rl* > *ḷḷ* does occur in the elicited data above. Cf. Midən 3.m.sg. *ḥəḷḷe*[26] and also in the texts below.

The verb *ḥoze – ḥzele (koḥoze)*

	sg.	pl.		
3.m.	*ḥzele*	*ḥzalle*	*koḥoze*	*koḥozən*
3.f.	*ḥzela*		*koḥəzyo*	
2.m.	*ḥzelox*	*ḥzalxu*	*koḥozat*	*koḥozutu*
2.f.	*ḥzelax*		*koḥozat*	
1.m.	*ḥzeli*	*ḥzelan*	*koḥozeno*	*koḥozina*
1.f.	*ḥzeli*		*koḥəzyono*	

Midən 2.m.sg. *ḥzéləx* (but in Jastrow 2002, 62 *ḥzelŭx*); 2.m.sg. *ḥozət;* 2.f.sg. *ḥəzyat.*[27]

The verb *maḥke – maḥkele (komaḥke)*

	sg.	pl.		
3.m.	*maḥkele*	*maḥkalle*	*komaḥke*	*komaḥkən*
3.f.	*maḥkela*		*komaḥᵊkyo*	
2.m.	*maḥkelox*	*maḥkalxu*	*komaḥkat*	*komaḥkutu*
2.f.	*maḥkelax*		*komaḥkat*	
1.m.	*maḥkeli*	*maḥkelan*	*komaḥkeno*	*komaḥkina*
1.f.	*maḥkeli*		*komaḥᵊyono*	

The verb *maḥət – maḥətle (komaḥət)*

	sg.	pl.		
3.m.	*maḥətle*	*maḥətte*	*komaḥət*	*komaḥti*
3.f.	*maḥətla*		*komaḥto*	
2.m.	*maḥətlox*	*maḥətxu*	*komaḥtat*	*komaḥtutu*

26 Cf. Talay 2004, 164.
27 Cf. Jastrow 1993, 66-67.

2.f.	*maḥətlax*		*komaḥtat*	
1.m.	*maḥətli*	*maḥətlan*	*komaḥətno*	*komaḥtina*
1.f.	*maḥətli*		*komaḥtono*	

The verb *omər – məḷḷe (komər)*

	sg.	pl.		
3.m.	*məṛle*	*məṛṛe*	*koməṛ*	*kəmmi*
3.f.	*məṛla*		*kəmmo*	
2.m.	*məṛlox*	*məṛxu*	*kəmmat*	*kəmmutu*
2.f.	*məṛlax*		*kəmmat*	
1.m.	*məṛli*	*məṛlan*	*komaṇṇo*	*kəmmina*
1.f.	*məṛli*		*kəmmono*	

The verb *maḥwe – maḥwele (komaḥwe)*

	sg.	pl.		
3.m.	*maḥwele*	*maḥwalle*	*komaḥwe*	*komaḥwən*
3.f.	*maḥwela*		*komaḥ^{ə}wiyo*	
2.m.	*maḥwelox*	*maḥwalxu*	*komaḥwat*	*komaḥwutu*
2.f.	*maḥwelax*		*komaḥwat*	
1.m.	*maḥweli*	*maḥwelan*	*komaḥwena*	*komaḥwina*
1.f.	*maḥweli*		*komaḥw^{i}yono*	

The verb *maqəm – maqəmle (komaqəm)*

	sg.	pl.		
3.m.	*maqəmle*	*maqəmme*	*komaqəm*	*komaqimi*
3.f.	*maqəmla*		*komaqimo*	
2.m.	*maqəmlox*	*maqəmxu*	*komaqimat*	*komaqimutu*
2.f.	*maqəmlax*		*komaqimat*	
1.m.	*maqəmli*	*maqəmlan*	*komaqəmno*	*komaqimina*
1.f.	*maqəmli*		*komaqimono*	

Midən 2.m.sg. *maqəmləx.*[28] 2.m.sg. *maqimət.*[29] *kmaqimat* may also is also attested.

The verb *mamṭe – mamṭele (komamṭe)*

	sg.	pl.		
3.m.	*mamṭele*	*mamṭalle*	*komamṭe*	*komamṭən*
3.f.	*mamṭela*		*komamṭ*ᵊ*yo*	
2.m.	*mamṭelox*	*mamṭalxu*	*komamṭat*	*komamṭutu*
2.f.	*mamṭelax*		*komamṭat*	
1.m.	*mamṭeli*	*mamṭelan*	*komamṭeno*	*komamṭina*
1.f.	*mamṭeli*		*komamṭiyono*	

The verb *maqbəl – maqbəle (komaqbəl)*

	sg.	pl.		
3.m.	*maqbele*	*maqballe*	*komaqbəl*	*komaq*ᵊ*bli*
3.f.	*maqbela*		*komaq*ᵊ*blo*	
2.m.	*maqbelox*	*maqbalxu*	*komaq*ᵊ*blat*	*komaq*ᵊ*blutu*
2.f.	*maqbelax*		*komaq*ᵊ*blat*	
1.m.	*maqbeli*	*maqbelan*	*komaqbanno*	*komaq*ᵊ*blina*
1.f.	*maqbeli*		*komaqbəlono*	

The verb *məǧǧəl – ǧǧil (koməǧǧəl)*

	sg.	pl.		
3.m.	*ǧǧil*	*ǧǧəlle* ~ *žǧili*	*koməǧǧəl*	*koməǧǧoli*
3.f.	*ǧǧilo*		*koməǧǧolo*	
2.m.	*ǧǧilat*	*ǧǧilutu* ~ *ǧǧəlxu*	*koməǧǧolat*	*koməǧǧolutu*
2.f.	*ǧǧilat*		*koməǧǧolat*	
1.m.	*ǧǧənno*	*ǧǧilina*	*koməǧǧanno*	*koməǧǧolina*
1.f.	*ǧǧilono*		*koməǧǧolono*	

---

28 Cf. Jastrow 1993, 100.
29 Cf. Jastrow 2002, 97.

In the elicited data also *kməğġanno* is attested.

The verb *nofəq – nafəq (konofəq)*

	sg.	pl.		
3.m.	*nafəq*	*nafiqi*	*konofəq*	*konəfqi*
3.f.	*nafiqo*		*konəfqo*	
2.m.	*nafiqăt*	*nafiqutu*	*konəfqat*	*konəfqutu*
2.f.	*nafiqăt*		*konəfqat*	
1.m.	*nafəqno*	*nafiqina*	*konofaqno*	*konəfqina*
1.f.	*nafiqono*		*konəfqono*	

The verb *obe – hule (kobe)*

	sg.	pl.		
3.m.	*hule*	*huwwe*	*kobe*	*kobən*
3.f.	*hula*		*kəbyo*	
2.m.	*hulox*	*huxu*	*kobat*	*kobutu*
2.f.	*hulax*		*kobat*	
1.m.	*huli*	*hulan*	*kobeno*	*kobina*
1.f.	*huli*		*kəbyono*	

Midən 2.m.sg. *huləx* (but in Jastrow 2002, 64 *hulŭx); 3.f.sg. ʾobo;* 2.m.sg. *ʾobət;* 1.f.sg. *ʾobono.*[30]

The verb *obəʿ - abəʿ (kobəʿ)*

	sg.	pl.		
3.m.	*abəʿ*	*abiʿi*	*kobəʿ*	*kəbʿi*
3.f.	*abiʿo*		*kəbʿo*	
2.m.	*abiʿat*	*abiʿutu*	*kəbʿat*	*kəbʿutu*
2.f.	*abiʿat*		*kəbʿat*	
1.m.	*abəʿno*	*abiʿina*	*kobaʿno*	*kəbʿina*
1.f.	*abiʿono*		*kəbʿono*	

30 Cf. Jastrow 1993, 65.

The verb *odəˁ - adəˁ (kodəˁ)*

	sg.	pl.		
3.m.	*adəˁ*	*adiˁi*	*kodəˁ*	*kədˁi*
3.f.	*adiˁo*		*kədˁo*	
2.m.	*adiˁat*	*adiˁutu*	*kədˁat*	*kədˁutu*
2.f.	*adiˁat*		*kədˁat*	
1.m.	*adəˁno*	*adiˁina*	*kodaˁno*	*kədˁina*
1.f.	*adiˁono*		*kədˁono*	

Midən 3.m.sg. *oḏəˁ - aḏəˁ*.[31] Father Akbulut pronounces it *ḏ* while in the elicited data the informant pronounced it *d*. This change maybe due to the informant's background.

The verb *qore – qrele (koqore)*

	sg.	pl.		
3.m.	*qrele*	*qralle*	*koqore*	*koqorən*
3.f.	*qrela*		*koqəryo*	
2.m.	*qrelox*	*qralxu*	*koqorat*	*koqorutu*
2.f.	*qrelax*		*koqorat*	
1.m.	*qreli*	*qrelan*	*koqoreno*	*koqorina*
1.f.	*qreli*		*koqəryono*	

The verb *soyəm – səmle (kosoyəm)*

	sg.	pl.		
3.m.	*səmle*	*səmme*	*kosoyəm*	*kosaymi*
3.f.	*səmla*		*kosaymo*	
2.m.	*səmlox*	*səmxu*	*kosaymat*	*kosaymutu*
2.f.	*səmlax*		*kosaymat*	
1.m.	*səmli*	*səmlan*	*kosoyamno*	*kosaymina*
1.f.	*səmli*		*kosaymono*	

Midən 2.m.sg. *səmləx* (but in Jastrow 2002, 64 *səmlŭx*); 2.m.sg. *saymət.*[32]

31 Cf. Jastrow 2002, 175.

The verb *ṣoxəṛ – ṣxəṛle (koṣoxəṛ)/ṣoxəṛ – ṣxəḷḷe (koṣoxəṛ)*

	sg.	pl.		
3.m.	*ṣxəṛle*	*ṣxəṛṛe*	*koṣoxəṛ*	*koṣəxṛi*
3.f.	*ṣxəṛla*		*koṣəxṛo*	
2.m.	*ṣxəṛlox*	*ṣxəṛxu*	*koṣəxṛat*	*koṣəxṛutu*
2.f.	*ṣxəṛlax*		*koṣəxṛat*	
1.m.	*ṣxəṛli*	*ṣxəṛlan*	*koṣoxaṛno*	*koṣəxṛina*
1.f.	*ṣxəṛli*		*koṣəxrono*	

Midən 3.m.sg. *ṣxəḷḷe.*[33]

The verb *šoməʿ - šaməʿ (košoməʿ)*

	sg.	pl.		
3.m.	*šaməʿ*	*šamiʿi*	*košoməʿ*	*košəmʿi*
3.f.	*šamiʿo*		*košəmʿo*	
2.m.	*šamiʿat*	*šamiʿutu*	*košəmʿat*	*košəmʿutu*
2.f.	*šamiʿat*		*košəmʿat*	
1.m.	*šaməʿno*	*šamiʿina*	*košomaʿno*	*košəmʿina*
1.f.	*šamiʿono*		*košəmʿono*	

Midən 2.m.sg. *šamiʿət.*[34]

The verb *yotu – yatu (koyotu)*

	sg.	pl.		
3.m.	*yatu*	*yatiwi*	*koyotu*	*koyətwi*
3.f.	*yatiwo*		*koyətwo*	
2.m.	*yatiwat*	*yatiwutu*	*koyətwat*	*koyətwutu*
2.f.	*yatiwat*		*koyətwat*	
1.m.	*yatəwno*	*yatiwina*	*koyotawno*	*koyətwina*
1.f.	*yatiwono*		*koyətwono*	

32 Cf. Jastrow 1993, 63-64.
33 Cf. Jastrow 2002, 179.
34 Cf. Jastrow 2002, 47.

The verb *qoṭəl – qṭile (koqoṭəl)*

	sg.	pl.		
3.m.	*qṭile*	*qṭəlle*	*koqoṭəl*	*koqəṭli*
3.f.	*qṭila*		*koqəṭlo*	
2.m.	*qṭilox*	*qṭəlxu*	*koqəṭlat*	*koqəṭlutu*
2.f.	*qṭilax*		*koqəṭlat*	
1.m.	*qṭili*	*qṭilan*	*koqoṭanno*	*koqəṭlina*
1.f.	*qṭili*		*koqəṭlono*	

Midən 2.m.sg. *qtiləx.*[35]

2.2.4 Transcription and translation

The transcription in this book follows the rules of transcription for Neo-Aramaic, Turoyo, used by Otto Jastrow in his Lehrbuch der Ṭuroyo-Sprache.[36] In general, preposition particles, such as *b-* "in, with" and *l-* "to, till, until" are separated from the word they refer to by hyphen (-), e.g.: *b-mən koməǧġolat?* "in what (language) do you speak?"; *aṯən l-gabi* "they came to me". The same applies also for the relative pronoun *d-*, e.g.: *u=qṭəl ʿamo d-hawi ʿal u=ʿamo səryoyo* "the genocide that came over the Syriac people". Hyphen is also used to separate the copula from the main word, e.g.: *naʿimo-yo* "he is little, small"; *barṯo-yo* "she is a girl, a daughter"; *mšiḥoye-ne* "they are Christians". Suffixes such as *-ze, -ste, -sti* or the long form *-stene* "also, too" is also separated from the main word by hyphen, e.g.: *lo=kəḏʿoli-ze* "she doesn't even know me"; *harke-ste* "also here"; *ba=kṯowe-sti* "also in the books"; *balki-stene …* "maybe also …".

The translation of the texts below is kept as close to source text as possible. In some few cases and because of comprehension difficulties, some phrases and sentences are rephrased. When needed, some clarification is given within parenthesis to facilitate the reading.

35 Cf. Jastrow 1993, 70.
36 Jastrow 2002.

3. Text 1

1. *ono kŭḏʿutu qašišo Yusəf Aqbuluṭ d-əDyarbakər di=Ndaṯalo d-Omiḏ, i=Ndaṯalo d-Omiḏ.*

2. *kŭḏʿutu hawi, i=šato da=tralfo, e hawi ṣbuṯo aʿmi, hawi măsăle*[37] *aʿmi, i=naqqa d-məḷḷi, d-məḷḷi, maqbeli u=sayfo, u=qṭəl ʿamo d-hawi ʿal u=ʿamo səryoyo w ʿal ann=armənoye.*

3. *maḥkewayli, aṯənwa ag=gazetat*[38] *mšayəlle mini, i=Hürryat, mšayəlle, məṛṛe, məṛṛe aṯən l-gabi məṛṛe: hat mək=kəmmat ʿal u=qṭul ʿamo dann=armənoye?*

4. *ono məḷḷi: aḥna harke=ʿitayḏan ʿito səryayto, aḥna səryoye-na harke. əmmi: ṭr=owe, hat xəd qašo, xəd kuhno, mək=kəmmat ʿal i=măsălaṯe?*

5. *omaṇṇo: ma man lo=koḏəʿ? ma man lo=koḏəʿ? hawi, hawi qṭul, qaṭlo, qṭəl ʿamo. hawi sayfo ʿal u=ʿamo, ʿal u=ʿamo armənoyo w ʿal u=səryoyo.*

6. *omaṇṇo: an=noše kŭlle kŭḏʿi. ŭʿdo kibŭx, d-omaṇṇo, ḥatta məḷḷi hawxa, omaṇṇo: ŭʿdo d-əmšaylat mu=ʿamo t-arke, d-əmmina ağlab mənne kito bam=mo balki*[39] *ḥamši kibŭx d-əmmat, u=ʿamo t-arke d-Dyarbakər, ya ğəddayye ya i=qaštaṯṯe mšiḥoye-ne mu=waxt du=sayfo.*

7. *u=ḥa d-hawi ṭayo, hawi, xaləṣ, fayəš, u=ḥa d-lo qṭəlwalle. hawxa-yo i=hnaṯṯe. m-awxa. ánnaqa ŭʿdo hənnək xliṭi b-ḥḏoḏe, kəmmi aḥna ğəddayna mšiḥoyo-yo, qaštayna mšiḥoye, m-awxa-yo. me tamo, mu=sayfo-yo.*

8. *e mərwayli ġălăbe medone tamo bag=gazetat. omaṇṇo: u=ḥa t.., yaʿni ono, əmmi: hat komaqbəlatle, tām*[40] *komaqbəlat u=medano? kobat hno, dastak?*[41] *omaṇṇo: e, komaqbaṇṇo w hawi u=medano.*

9. *hənnək-si*[42] *kṯuwwe me d-məḷḷi kṯuwwe w ḥatta məḷḷi, omaṇṇo: i=naqlayo hənnək əmmiwa, am=mallawataṯṯi əmmiwa, əmmiwa: u=ḥa d-qoṭəl šawʿo mšiḥoye gəzzé li=malkuṯo. hŭl lu=medano məḷḷi.*

---

37 Cf. Tur. *mesele* "issue, matter, problem".
38 Cf. Tur. *gazete* "newspaper".
39 Cf. Tur. *belki* "perhaps, maybe".
40 Cf. Tur. *tam* "whole, full, complete, perfect".
41 Cf. Tur. *destek* "encouragement, permission" and Kur. *destek* "support".
42 *-si, -se, -ze, -ste, -sti* and the long form *-stene* "also, too" Cf. Jastrow 1978, 301 and Jastrow 1992, 178 and 184. Cf. also Talay 2004, 188.

10. *w omanno: yaʿni ono, ono šaməʿwayno ġălăbe medone aṣāṣ meqəm-ste šaməʿwayno, ono i=yemo d-babi ono me ʿIwardo-no-ste, yaʿni xəd məlli, i=yemo d-babi ḥzela u=sayfo, hiya ʿayišóle.*

11. *maḥkiyowa, kŭl=gave*[43] *maḥkiyowa eli w lan=naʿime, ŭmmowa hawxa w hawxa saymiwa appe w qəṭlənwanne w bəʿğənwanne ba=.., bu=dexono w bah=hne, saymiwanne qáflat*[44] *quṭliwanne, məbliwanne.*

12. *ánnaqla mərwayli hate lah=hne-ste, l-ani, lag=gazğatiyye*[45] *di=Hürriyet d-atən-sti. omanno: saymiwanne harke kəmmila qafla hēš, yaʿni u=hno du=.., du=ʿamo di=naqla du=qṭəl ʿamo.*

13. *saymiwa u=ʿamo qafle məbliwalle, qəṭlənwanne w otənwa məbliwa hēš. ánnaqqa hēš kəmmila qafle hawxa, bu=lešono tərki, kəmmila qaf.., qaflá, qaflá zama.., u=waxt di=qaflá kəmmile.*

14. *ánnaqqa ono mərwayli aqqa medonani bag=gazetat u, e xəd məlli yaʿni, xəd kŭdʿutu, u, w ono, ono kodaʿno u=medano d-hawi w šaməʿno mi=yemo d-babi maḥkelalan ġălăbe medone u qreli ba=ktowe-sti, qreli u=medano hawxa-yo.*

15. *ánnaqqa mə=d-maḥətte bah=hne, bag=gazetat, ba=sfar yawme ṭr=owe, bətər, bətər b-yawmo nafiqi, deri yawmo nafiqo bi=.., bi=gazeta.*

16. *hedi*[46] *hawi ʿasṛiyye xŭd ŭʿdo, hawi ʿasṛiyye b-lalyo, atən, atən ap=polis atən l-arke polis, səfil*[47] *polis, yaʿni d-kolawši səfil, ğule səfil. w atən l-arke əmmi: tŭx, tŭx u=mŭdūraydan*[48] *koqorelŭx, u=mŭdūr di=yamniyye*[49] *dap=polis, u=rabo d-Dyarbakər yaʿni.*

17. *hedi i=naqlayo zəḥto-wa, məbliwa an=noše qəṭliwanne əmmiwa: noše lə=gdəʿ ma=qṭilile. hənnək məbliwa an=noše qəṭliwanne əmmiwa: noše lə=gdəʿ ma=qṭilile. kətwa zəḥto ġălăbe.*

18. *ono məlli alle, hawxa ati medano l-boli, omanno, kito zəḥto, əmmina, omanno: ma ṣafro d-oteno b-imomo lə=kowe? əmmi: lo; əʿdo gdotat aʿmayna! əmmi: u=mŭdūr kokolelŭx! əʿdo xayifo glozəm d-otat.*

19. *qayəm ono-sti məlli, omanno: ma zət, mede ma zət-tər*[50] *mu=mawto layto, ʿar-ruḥi məlli. omanno: mede, mawto-yo, zət-tər mu=mawto layt mede ḥreno.*

---

43 Cf. Kur. *gav* "instant, moment, time".
44 Cf. Tur. *kafile* "caravan" and Kur. *qefle* "herd".
45 Cf. Tur. *gazeteci* "journalist".
46 Cf. Kur. *êdî* "then".
47 Cf. Tur. *sivil* "civil".
48 Cf. Tur. *müdür* "chief, head, direcor".
49 Cf. Tur. *emniyet* "security".
50 *-tər* comparative suffix "more".

20. *azzino lwəšli ğuli, azzí ʿam ap=polis. mḥeli ʿal u=tarʿo du=mŭdūr, maṭina l-su=mŭdūr*[51] *mḥeli ʿal u=tarʿayde̱. ati̱ l-qamuti̱ omər̥: oh, tŭx, hawxa yaʿni bə-fṣiḥuto̱ hne, xəd dəmmat, maḥwele hno aʿmi.*

21. *ati̱ l-qamuti̱, yatiwina ğğilina. omər̥: komaḥwe m-idə̱t latwaylan ġălăbe, hano u=mŭdūr, komaḥwe om.., m-idə̱t latwaylan aḥna, ono w hat ġălăbe asiruto̱, diyalōġ*[52] *ʿam əḥdode, u=medano hawi, səmlŭx. omanṇo: komanṇo e, baʿ e. kmaḥwe hawxa may=koda̱ʿno, hawxa ono-sti mede.*

22. *hiye zbəṭle, qayem yatiwina side, zbəṭle b-maẓḅaṭa,*[53] *kəmminala yaʿni, maẓḅaṭa, b-ḥaqq didi̱, yaʿni qay məḷḷi u=medano w qay ğġənno medone hawxa. zbəṭle b-maẓḅaṭa b-ḥaqq didi̱. mər̥le, mšayele, mšayele, omər̥: hatu m-ayko-hatu?*

23. *omanṇo: aḥna u=ʿamo, mšayele ʿal u=ʿamo səryoyo, omər̥: hatu m-ayko-hatu? omanṇo: aḥna u=ʿamo ʿatiqo d-Be̱t Nahrin-na, u=ʿamo ʿatiqo d-Məzopəṭᵒmya. noše ʿatəq-tər minan layto harke. w aḥna i=dŭkṯayda̱n harke-yo.*

24. *w ono mə=d-məḷḷi hawxa ʿayəqle hiye, lo=rḥəmle qay yaʿni komanṇo i=dŭkṯayda̱n harke-yo w u=hnayda̱n harke-yo.*

25. *ḥəḷḷi koʿoyaqle, omanṇo: hăka*[54] *lə=gmətyaqnat tŭx aḥna kətlan ʿito, i=ʿito t-koweno eba hawila tralfo=šne, waxta t-kowela tralfo=šne d-maʿməralle w d-kətwa ʿamo səryoyo harke. w i=ʿito das=səryoye-yo. ono hawxa mə́ḷḷile. omər̥: lo? omanṇo: e bele, tŭx əḥzay!*

26. *axə́r mədle u=nufusaydi̱,*[55] *yaʿni kṯule zbəṭle b-maẓḅaṭa. w mərwayli ġălăbe medone tamo bi=maẓḅaṭa. mə=d-əmšayele mə́ḷḷile.*

27. *fayəšno gabayye. mə=d-hawyo i=saʿa traḥṣar mkamele i=maẓḅaṭa, hano u=mŭdūr di=yamniyye. omər̥: zŭx ytaw tamo, yaʿni hano kəmmile taḥt-i=ʿayno.*

28. *azzí kalino tamo bayn ap=polis hul, kalino gabayye hŭl ṣafro hawxa, yaʿ.., qimo w hno baynoṯayye w aʿmayye.*

29. *hēš i=saʿa hawyo ḥdo du=lalyo, omanṇo kfotaḥno tălăfōn lu=bayto gdomanṇo, gdomanṇo: kalí raḥa-no w layt mede d-lo=saymutu, d-lo=wuto bi=məṭṭala.*

30. *azzən mər̥r̥e lu=mŭdūr omər̥: ṭr̥=owe. omər̥: ṭro fotəḥ. omər̥: ŭʿdo d-lo gšəmʿo briṯo kula, an=noše kŭlle, kŭlle kšəmʿi kalé u=qašo zbiṭ w lo=kəḏ.., be məğ=ğarile, ksaymi maraq.*[56]

51 The preposition *se-* "by, at" is shortend to *s-* before the definit article, Cf. Jastrow 1993, 261.

52 Cf. Tur. *diyalog* "dialog".

53 Cf. Tur. *mazbata* "petition, protocol".

54 Cf. Kur. *heke* "if".

55 Cf. Tur. *nüfus (cüzdanı)* "identification card".

56 Cf. Tur. *merak* "concern, anxiety".

31. *qayəm ftəḥle omər̤: mar̤li i=număra! məḻḻi i=număra du=bayto, ftəḥle tălăfōn lu=bayto, l-arke gaban. omər̤, ğġənno ʿam u=bayto b-səryoyo, ğġənno ʿam u=bayto b-səryoyo ḥa mənne ṣxər̤le u=tălăfōn. mədle m-iḏi. ṣxər̤le u=tălăfōn qumi, mər̤le: uhm … məs=səmlelŭx.*[57]

32. *omaṉṉo: hat qay hawxa kosaymat? hawxa xəd əqḥəṉṉo, qḥəṉṉo, tabi hno polis-wayne, qḥəṉṉo, omaṉṉo: qay hawxa kosaymat?*

33. *omər̤: hat b-mən koməğġolat? omaṉṉo: koməğġanno b-səryoyo. mək=kəmmat? komaṉṉo: kalí raḥa-no w layt mede, ʿam u=baytaḏi, ʿam i=qarṯayḏi. omər̤, omər̤, qḥir, omər̤: hat áydarbo gməğġolat səryoyo bu=bayto? məš=šəkəl gməğġolat səryoyo?*

34. *omaṉṉo: baʿ b-mən gməğġanno? omaṉṉo: ono səryoyo-no. aṯutu mi=ʿito mbalxŭli w aḻo səryoyo koməğġolina bu=bayto w b-səryoyo komṣalina w səryoye-na ḥna. omaṉṉo: u=lešonayḏan hano-yo! omaṉṉo: lešono ʿatiqo; ʿatəq-tər mine lešone layt, d-mšiḥo.*

35. *hiye qḥir ġălăbe, omər̤: qay bu=bayto gməğġolat sər.., səryoyo w lə=ğġilat, lə=gməğġolat tərki? omaṉṉo: hawxa? omər̤: e. omaṉṉo, qḥənno, omaṉṉo: hăka, hăka ha-sti,*[58] *omaṉṉo šr̤olo gawro ṭawwo-hat, iyzŭx kalé Dyarbakər u=gunaydoġu*[59] *kule koməğġəl b-, b-kŭrmanği. iyzŭx lo=ṭorat məğġoli kŭrmānği! ʿayn hawxa mắḻḻile.*

36. *hiye-sti omər̤ hedi, kali, law aḏəʿ mə=d-omər̤. kali, law aḏəʿ mə=d-omər̤. hedi ono-sti omaṉṉo: hat komaḥwe lo=kəḏʿat, qḥəṉṉo mine, omaṉṉo: lo=kəḏʿat ʿam man, məš=šəkəl ksaymat hno, maʿmala,*[60] *hno yaʿni, e.*

37. *hedi hawxa kalina hŭl ṣafro gabayye. u=mŭdūr-sti, u=mŭdūr-sti hawi ṣafro, lo, edi bəṯər omər̤, omər̤: ftaḥ! omər̤: ftaḥ məğġal b-tərki ʿam u=bayto.*

38. *ftəḥle, ftəḥle u=tălăfōn disa*[61] *ğġənno b-tərki ʿam u=bayto. omaṉṉo, e omaṉṉo, omaṉṉo, omaṉṉo: əʿdo gməğġanno ʿam i=payrayḏi*[62] *b-tərki lo=kə.., ġălăbe mede hno, nŭxroyo-yo, lo=kəḏʿoli-ze, balki lo=məğġolo aʿmi-ze, omaṉṉo.*

39. *omər̤: ftaḥ məğġal qana*[63] *d-, qana d-ədʿina ḥna-sti mək=kəmmat, mək=kosaymat, mən əhno. hedi ftəḥle ğġənno b-tərki ʿam u=bayto. omaṉṉo: kalí ṭawwo-no layt mede, lo=saymutu mṭala w hawxa.*

---

57 Mispronunciation *məs=səmlŭx* "what have you done" is expected.
58 Cf. *hatə-sti* "you also".
59 Cf. Tur. *güneydoğu* "southeast".
60 Cf. Tur. *muamele* "behavior".
61 Cf. Kur. *dîsa* "again".
62 Cf. Kur. *pîr* "old".
63 *qana* introduces final clauses and it is attested five times in this material. *žboyəd* is used for the same purpose and is attested twice in the material.

40. *hedi fayəšno hŭl ṣafro tamo. i=saᶜa hawyo ḥamməš u falga ṣafrayto aṯi u=mŭdūr omər̤: qəm! mə́r̤l̤eli, omər̤: qəm păpāz*[64] *afandi,*[65] *ṣafrayto. omər̤: qəm hawat mašhūr.*[66] *hawxa mə́r̤l̤eli.*

41. *de, omaṉṉo: ṭraylŭx-lo, hawxa qḥənno, b-qaḥăr. omər̤: qəm iyzŭx, tro tre polis tro mublilŭx lu=bayto. omaṉṉo: lo! hawxa b-, qḥənno. omaṉṉo: gəzzí ono. omər̤: məš=šəkəl gəzzŭx? omaṉṉo: gəzzí áydarbo t-owe. omər̤: lo, lo, tro mublilŭx.*

42. *aṯən mṭallali lu=bayto. aṯina lu=bayto i=saᶜa hawyo ḥamməš komqarawla laš=šēṯ ṣafro. aṯino omaṉṉo gdomaxno čike. lə=ṭralle d-domaxno tamo. omaṉṉo gdomaxno čike. daməxno əšmo, tarte saᶜayat. i=saᶜa hawyo tmone ḥəl̤l̤i əmmi: tŭx, disa u=polis koqorelŭx. aṯən ánnaqa disa ap=polis.*

43. *mən-yo? əmmi: tŭx ánnaqa koqorelŭx hano, kəmminale u=ğ.., u=ṣawği,*[67] *ğumhuriyat*[68] *dawlat*[69] *güwanlək*[70] *maḥkămasi*[71] *ṣaw.., du=ṣawği, u=rabo di=hno, di=maḥkăma ánnaqa. hayo i=măsăle yariwo w ... omaṉṉo: ṭr=owe.*

44. *qayəm disa lwəšli ğuli azzí d-əzzí ᶜam ap=polis, ap=polis əmmi: ma hēš lo=nafiqat larwal harke? omaṉṉo: lo, lo=nafəqno. omaṉṉo: qay? əmmi: kalé at=tălăfəzyōne w ag=gazetat w ah=hne d-əbriṯo kula kalə́n qmə-u=tarᶜo, kəbᶜi d-gurši ṣərṭo elŭx. omaṉṉo: lə=.., maṉṉo: ṭro gurši; ġamo layt. u=polis omər̤: lo! lo=maqbele. lə=ṭrele d-gurši.*

45. *hedi i=naqqlayo hənnək kətwa ḥamšo polis-wayne, sfil. azzən tre mənne makralle*[72] *u=ᶜamo w ag=gazəğatiyye w at=tălăfəzyōne, makranne*[73] *tamo b-dŭkṯo. ğğile hawxa maġġəlanne. ono-sti maᶜraqalli, mahzammali tamo-da, b-dŭkṯo ḥreto-da mofəqalli hŭl li=ğaᶜda,*[74] *mi=ᶜito.*

46. *mər̤r̤e, makralle ḥa taqsi*[75] *ma-š=šaᶜuṯe mər̤r̤e, mər̤r̤e: taqsi klay! mər̤r̤e: hano maḥkūm-yo.*[76] *mər̤r̤e: el.., hano maḥkūm-yo. mə́r̤r̤alle hawxa qana d-l=obən d-l=obən kallawat lu=taqsi.*

64 Cf. Tur. *papaz* "priest, minister, pastor".
65 Cf. Tur. *efendi* "mister, gentelman".
66 Cf. Tur. *meşhur* "famous".
67 Cf. Tur. *savcı* "prosecutor".
68 Cf. Tur. *cumhuriyet* "republic".
69 Cf. Tur. *devlet* "state".
70 Cf. Tur. *guvenlık* "security".
71 Cf. Tur. *mahkeme* "court".
72 Mispronunciation *maklanne* "stopped them" is expected.
73 Mispronunciation *maklanne* "stopped them" is expected.
74 Cf. Tur. *cadde* "street".
75 Cf. Tur. *taksi* "taxi".
76 Cf. Tur. *mahkûm* "sentenced, condemned".

47. *mballali li=hno, mballali li=maḥkăma tamo. azzino yatuno, ap=polis kanne*[77] *aʿmi. u=ṣawği, hano d-ánnaqqa, ánnaqqa kḥoyanno omər: me qime gdobat i=yfada!*[78]

48. *omaṇṇo b-qaḥăr, omaṇṇo: áydarbo d-əbʿat hawxa. ono qḥə́rwayno. fayəš ġălăbe ʿağəzwayno u omaṇṇo mən d-howe gdomaṇṇo mən d-oṯe qəm femi gdomaṇṇo, law ... hīč*[79] *haw ksamno tə=hno.*

49. *qayəm koqore i=yfada d-hiwoli ʿasṛiyye kula, b-lalyo, i=yfadayo kula koqorela. komər: haṯe hat hulŭx i=yfadaṯe? omaṇṇo: e, ono hiwoli. omər: kito mede ḥreno d-maḥtat aʿla? omaṇṇo: e. omaṇṇo: kito mede ḥreno d-maḥənno aʿla.*

50. *ánnaqla i=naqlayo kṯuwalle aʿli bag=gazetat t-Turkya harke "u=xayin*[80] *d-baynoṯayna!". u kətwa u=ṣlibo-sti b-iḏi, b-i.., ḥzalle, balki ḥzallŭx bi=hno. məṛṛe: "u=xayin d-baynoṯayna". mən-yo, qana d-oṯe d-noše d-qoṭeli-sti! hŭl li=dărăğayo.*[81]

51. *maḥtalle "u=xayin d-baynoṯayna", yaʿni kŭlle ṭaye-ne, ono ḥa ono bass ṣuroyo u qašo maqbeli u=qṭ.., u=sayfo, u=qṭəl ʿamo dann=armənoye w das=səryoye. məḷḷi: me kule lebi komaṇṇo w kmaqbanno w hawi.*

52. *ánnaqqa žboyəd*[82] *d-oṯe ḥa d-qoṭeli hawxa səmme hno, maḥətte hno tamo. ánnaqla qrele, qrele i=hno, hano, u=.., ifada, qəryole d-hiwoli kula. omər: kīt mede ḥreno d-əmmat? omaṇṇo: e. omaṇṇo: tamo maḥətte aʿli məṛṛe eli xayin tamo!*

53. *omaṇṇo: aḥna ʿamo səryoyo. omaṇṇo: hani bann=alfowat əšne, omaṇṇo kalán harke koʿayšina w ʿam Turkya, ʿam i=dawla me zawno, me dore yarixe kalán ʿam i=dawla t-Turkya koʿayšina. w aḥna ʿamo ṭawwo ʿam i=dawla.*

54. *bass i=dawla, i=dawla t-Turkya lo=kəḏʿo i=.., l=aḏiʿo i=qimayḏan. d-əmmina l=aḏiʿo bu=qadrayḏan ət-kə́twayna hawxa ʿamo ṭawwo, t-kə́twayna hno, t-kə́twaylan, d-əmmina kŭltūr,*[83] *d-kə́twaylan mede hno. l=aḏiʿo i=qimayḏan. omaṇṇo: aḥna kosaymina ʿaskariyye, kobina văgi,*[84] *ko.., aḥna mə=t.., mə=t-kolozəm kosaymina laf i=dawla.*

---

77 Cf. *kalə́nne* "here they are".
78 Cf. Tur. *ifade* "testimony".
79 Cf. Tur. *hiç* "nothing, none whatsoever".
80 Cf. Tur. *hain* "traitor".
81 Cf. Tur. *derece* "degree".
82 Cf. Kur. *jibo* "for, for the sake of".
83 Cf. Tur. *kültür* "culture".
84 Cf. Tur. *vergi* "taxes".

55. *bass ono mə́ṛṛali harke xayə.., kəmmili xayin! omaṇṇo: kṯaw tamo u=ḥa d-mə́ṛḷeli xayin, xayin hiye-yo. hedi kṯule hawo-sti tamo, maḥətle ʿal i=hnayo u ... hedi bəṯərke qayəm oməṛ, aṯən tre polis disa mṭallali lu=bayto. hedi huwwali li=maḥkăma.*

56. *i=maḥkăma ṭləbbe eli šēṯ, me arbaʿ=əšne hŭl šēṯ=əšne ḥăpəs. i=dăʿwa*[85] *komaḷḷa tlaṯmo=traḥṣar, tlaṯmo=traḥṣar. d-əmmina d-ḥa folaġ u=ʿamo, d-əmmina d-folaġno ʿamo, xəd folaġno u=ʿamo səryoyo maqəmne mqabəl di=dawla t-Turkya, mede hawxa.*

57. *tlaṯmo, i=dăʿwa kəmmila tlaṯmo=traḥṣar. ono me arbaʿ=əšne hŭl šēṯ=əšne huwwali ḥăpəs, xəd məḷḷi, ṭləballi yaʿni. e hedi huwwali l-i=maḥkăma.*

58. *i=maḥkăma, kŭḏʿuto, aṯən, mi=maḥkăma, aṯiwa ʿamo ġălăbe me, mu=Swed, w me, me Almaniya-sti aṯiwa u kətwa, w ʿamo, yaʿni kətwa, kətwa baynoṯayye mu=parlamanto*[86] *du=Swed kətwa noše w kətwa me hani zədqe nušoye, inṣān ḥaqlări,*[87] *zədqe nušoye kəmminanne, awrəp.., d-Awroppa aṯənwa hənnək-sti.*

59. *w ḥatta i=naqqayo lu=ğumhūr bašqāni*[88] *d-Almanya hiye-sti kṯuwwayle maktūb aʿmayye eli, lăğani mšadarle: kṭəlbinalŭx šlomo w kṭəlbinalŭx hno ... hawxa medone kṯuwwayle bu=maktūbayḏe.*

60. *w aṯən l-arke aʿmi hŭl li=maḥkăma, hŭl li=maḥkăma qamayto w ġălăbe haṯe maḥwela hno rabo, d-əmmina ḥaylo rabo. Turkya zayiʿo d-əmmat. aṯən hani kŭlle li=maḥkăma aʿmi, i=naqqa d-azzí li=maḥkăma.*

61. *u=ḥakəm mədle qrele i=gazetayo di=Hürriyat t-kətwa u=ṣlibo b-idi, oməṛ: hat, mšayele mini, w hənnək kŭlle ʿabiri li=maḥkăma, hani d-aṯan kəppale arbʿi šaxṣat, ḥamši balki, omər, oməṛ: kalé qqoreno*[89] *hat məḷḷŭx am=medonani kŭlle? mədle qrele i=Hürriyet. omaṇṇo: e, hani kŭlle ğğilinanne, mirili maḥtile tamo, kṯiwile tamo.*

62. *hedi boṯər mi=naqqayo mtaxrarre i=dăʿwa ḥz... ḥzalle d-əmmina aṯi ʿamo ġălăbe m-Awrəppa mtaxralle. w i=naqqa dat=tarte-sti disa, disa qrallali li=maḥkăma. disa a=sniġrayḏi, yaʿni u=mede d-lazəm məṛṛe lo=hnalle ... w ono-sti u=mede d-lazəm yaʿni lo=daʿəṇṇo w lo=daʿəṇṇo bi=.., bu=mede d-məḷḷi.*

63. *w hedi dat=tlaṯ-si*[90] *hawxa. hedi bəṯər hiye hawiwa ġălăbe mu=ʿamayḏan, noše mšaylone d-əmmina, ġălăbe mšayəlle d-əmmina maḥwalle ḥaylo rabo.*

---

85 Cf. Tur. *dava* “trial, lawsuit, allegation”.
86 Cf. Tur. *parlamento* “parliament”.
87 Cf. Tur. *insan hakları* “human rights”.
88 Cf. Tur. *cumhur/devlet başkanı* “president”.
89 *qqoreno* < **kqoreno* “I read”.
90 Cf. *-sti*.

u=ʿamaydan kule d-Awrəppa maḥwalle ḥaylo rabo, yaʿni xŭd kŭḏʿutu balki b-Almanya kətwa balki ḥamšo=što alfo šaxṣat ṣayəm yawmo w səmme hno mqabəl t-Turkya.

64. *hani kŭlle mṭanne maḥwallan, maḥwallan li=hno, lu=.., lu=ḥakəm*[91] *harke, kalé hawxa-yo i=măsăle w u=ʿamo kule bəṯr i=măsălaṯe-yo w bəṯr u=qašo-yo w layto hno.*

65. *hedi zayiʿo p-hawxa lo=.., lə=ḥkəmlali, hiye u=.., u=.., xəd komaṇṇo hiye u=qonṣoloṣ-sti,*[92] *u=qonṣoloṣ d-Ameriqa-sti mšayewayle mini d-Ameriqa mšayewele mini, omər: ma mḥallalŭx? márṛalŭx mede?*

66. *omaṇṇo: lo=mḥallali bass ʿal d-məğğol.., ʿal d-koməğğoliwayna səryoyo bu=bayto ḥa mənne mʿanatle hawxa aʿmi, qḥir. məṛle: qay koməğğolat səryoyo bu=bayto? mərwayli am=medonani kŭlle lu=qonṣolōṣ-sti w hawxa.*

67. *w kətwa hiye mu=ʿamaydan-sti kətwa hən yaʿni zayiʿiwa, d-əmmina d-əṣṭanbəl, am=mərdnoye. ġălăbe, ġălăbe zayiʿiwa məṛṛe: dʿaṛ eba. məṛṛe, məṛṛe: dʿaṛ əmdagal u=mede d-məḷḷŭx əmdagele bag=.., bag=gazetat, bat=tălăfəzyōne.*

68. *ono məḷḷi: lo=, lo=kəmdaganno, laybi mdaganno. w mərwayli xəd məḷḷi ba=hne-sti, bag=gazetat-sti awwəl naqqla d-nafiqowa, ono məḷḷi: ono kuhno-no lo=kəmdaganno w lə=kwe d-əmdaganno. u=medano šṛolo-yo w hawxa-yo w hawxa tamo-sti məḷḷi hawxa-yo yaʿni, hīč lo=daʿəṇṇo eba w məḷḷi.*

69. *u kətwa hən mu=ʿamaydan ġălăbe hnewalle, ġălăbe kətwa hən zayiʿiwa, d-əmmina d-kətne zangin,*[93] *d-kətne hne. kətwa ḥa məṛle, omər ftəḥleli tălăfōn, omər: moqadlŭxlan, moqadlŭxlan, hawxa məṛle: moqadlŭxlan. áydarbo gsaymət mede hawxa?*

70. *omaṇṇo: lo? ma məs=səmli ma gmoqadlŭx? omər: lo=kowe d-əmmat medone mani! omaṇṇo: məḷḷi w azzeyo. omaṇṇo: məḷḷi w azzeyo. u=mede d-məḷḷi məḷḷi w azzeyo. haw kodoʿəṛ, omaṇṇo.*

71. *e omər, omər: gəmšaḏaṇṇo u=tălăfəzyōn gabŭx maṛ, mdagal i=măsăle maṛ falan! omaṇṇo: laybi samno mede hawxa. u=mede d-məḷḷi šṛolo-yo! ono u=wuždānaydi*[94] *raḥat-yo.*[95] *šṛolo məḷḷi w hawxa-yo.*

72. *w hedi hawxa, yaʿni ġălăbe mu=ʿamaydan maḥwewalle hno mqabəl … bass yaʿni u=ʿamaydan kŭl=gave komaškaṇṇe, yaʿni bi=măsălayo ġălăbe. ġălăbe tawdi l-kŭlle, yaʿni d-maḥwalle ḥaylo ġălăbe rabo bi=hnaṯe.*

---

91 Cf. Tur. *hakem* "judge".
92 Cf. Tur. *konsolos* "consul".
93 Cf. Tur. *zengin* "rich, wealthy".
94 Cf. Tur. *vicdan* "conscience".
95 Cf. Tur. *rahat* "calm".

73. *w haṯe măsăle hawyo-wa ġălăbe rapṯo aṣaṣan. yaʿni xəd məḷḷi, xəd məṛle mə́ṛṛalle*[96] *bu=tălăfəzyōn-sti haṯe latwa i=măsălayḏi w bass d-əmmina, i=măsăle du=ʿamo səryoyo kule, du=ʿamayḏan du=mšiḥoyo kule-yo haṯe.*

74. *haṯe i=naqqa d-əqṭiḷənne lo=məṛṛe: hani bass qquṭḷina;*[97] *qṭəlle u=ʿamo, ayna d-maṭ.., u=ʿamo mšiḥoyo kule qṭəlle. d-qədṛiwa gəmkamliwa kule.*

75. *e yaʿni haṯe balki, d-əmmina m-Aḷoho-wa, balki i=naqqa d-əmšayele mini ono, hən, hən mu=ʿamo məṛṛe: mdagal i=măsăle. i=naqqa d-əmšayele mini u=ḥakəm, oməṛ, oməṛ, ono yaʿni hawxa mṣawər qull ʿayni, omaṇṇo: aʿu, omaṇṇo: áydarbo gdomaṇṇo lawi u=medano yaʿni ono lo=maqbele u=wuždānayḏi, lo=hnele.*

76. *omaṇṇo haqqa qṭəlle ʿamo, haqqa qṭəlle, quṭḷiwa yaʿni kuhne, ḥasye, dayroye hīč lo=maṛḥimiwa appe, áydarbo gdomaṇṇo lawi mede hawxa. omaṇṇo, omaṇṇo: e hawi, mə=d-kowe ṭṛ=owe omaṇṇo.*

77. *zət-tər mu=mawto? omaṇṇo u=mede t-səmme səmme eban, yaʿni hawxa məfakaḷḷi, u=mede t-səmme səmme, zət-tər mawxa law kəppe saymi. omaṇṇo: ṭṛowe, ṭṛo saymi-sti. yaʿni hawi. hawi, šṛoḷo-yo.*

78. *w hawxa yaʿni xəd kŭḏʿutu šmīʿ yaʿni bə-briṯo kula. ono mərwayli bag=gazetat-sti, omaṇṇo: gmašmaʿno qoli bə-briṯo kula, u ku.., koṭəlbina u=ḥaqqayḏan. qay q.., aḥna d-lo sūğ*[98] *w d-lo săbab*[99] *qṭəlallan, maḥətte, mṭalle sayfo aʿlayna ʿayn hawxa mətfakarwayno ono yaʿni.*

79. *ġălăbe noše-sti, lə=gbaʿno d-omaṇṇo ann=əšmonaṯṯe-sti d-əmmina d-məṛṛe: dʿaṛ eba. kətwa hən kuhne, kətwa hən ʿamo, kətwa hən məṛṛe: qquṭḷilŭx.*[100] *kətwa hən d-məṛṛe, məṛṛe: qquṭḷilŭx kṣuxṛi i=ʿito.*

80. *ono məḷḷi omaṇṇo: ṭṛo-quṭḷili, lanno*[101] *ṭaw manək kŭlle d-əqṭili. ṭṛo ṣuxri i=ʿito. hăka ʿal foṯi d-məṣxoṛo i=ʿito ṭṛ=qəṭ.., ṣuxṛila. ma i=ʿito layba … qay ma hno-yo gṣuxṛi i=ʿito. e hawxa yaʿni, hawxa-yo.*

81. *e tlaṯ kore yaʿni ḥkəmmallı bı=maḥkăma rapṯo d-, d-Dyarbakər t-Turkya yaʿni. tlaṯ kore ʿal d-məḷḷi qṭil u=ʿamo səryoyo, aṯi sayfo aʿle u, w hawxa yaʿni.*

---

96 *miṛalle* “they said it” is expected here.
97 The future prefix *g* is assimilated, *qquṭḷina* < **gquṭḷina* “we will murder”.
98 Cf. Tur. *suç* “guilt, fault, blame”.
99 Cf. Tur. *sebep* “reason”.
100 Cf. **gquṭḷilŭx* “they will murder you”.
101 Cf. *latno* “I am not”.

4. Translation text 1

1. As you know, I am father Yusuf Akbulut from Diyarbakir, from the (church of the) Virgin Mary of Omid,[102] the Virgin Mary of Omid.
2. You know that in year 2000 there was this occurrence, this happening when I said, I said that I admit the Sayfo,[103] the massacre, the killing of the Syriac people and the Armenians.
3. I told, the (Turkish) newspaper, Hurriyet came and asked me and said: what do you think of the massacre of the Armenian people?
4. I said: our church here is a church, we are Syriacs here. They said: nevertheless, you as priest, a church person, what do you say in this matter?
5. I said: who doesn't know? Who doesn't know? There was a killing, a slaughter, an ethnic cleansing. There was a massacre, of the Armenian people and the Syriac people.
6. I said: everyone knows. You may now ask the people living here (in Diyarbakir), the majority of them, maybe fifty percent of them have either a grandfather or a grandmother that is originally Christian, from the time of the massacre, also this I told them.
7. The one that converted to Islam, he converted, he stayed alive, he was saved, and the one that did not he was killed. Thus is their, how should I say it. This is why. And now when they all are mixed together they say our grandfather is Christian, our grandmother is Christian. It is because of that. That is the reason. It is from the time of the massacre.
8. So I had said lots of things there, in the newspapers. I said: the one that ..., they said: do you believe it? Do you totally believe this? Do you support this (statement)? I said: yes I believe and it (of course) happened.
9. And they wrote down everything that I said. I also said: furthermore, at that time (at the time of the massacre) they used to say, their mullahs used to say that everyone that kills seven Christians will go to heaven, also this I said.

---

102 This is the Turoyo name of the city of Diarbakir.
103 Sayfo "sword" is the term used for the massacres of 1915.

10. And I said, I had earlier heard lots of things (about the massacres), I am originally from ʿIwardo, and my grandmother witnessed and survived the massacre (so I had heart a lot).

11. She used to tell, very often she told me and the other children that they (the Turks and the Kurds) did this and that to them (the Christians), they killed them and choked them with smoke and so on. They used to gather them in *qaflat,* (groups), took them away and killed them.

12. So I had said also this to the, to these, to the journalists from Hurriyet, that had come to me, I said: they used to gather them in *qaflat*; they still use the term *qaflat* here, referring to killing of people, the massacre.

13. They used to gather a group of people, take them away, massacre them and come back to take more. So they still, until this day say *qafle* (a group) in Turkish. They say *qafla* epoch, it is known as the epoch of *qafla*.

14. So I had said all this in the newspapers and as I said, as you know, I know that this took place and I also heard from my grandmother and read in the books about it, I read that this happened.

15. So when they put this in the newspapers, in the newspapers, after one day, after one day it was published, the day after it (my statement) was in the newspaper.

16. So, when it became evening, just like now evening, night, they came, the police came here, police, civil police, those are dressed in civil, civil clothes. They came here and said: come, come our chief asks for you, the police chief of security, the chief of Diyarbakir, so to say.

17. That time was a time of fear. They (the police) used to drag people away, kill them and say that no one knows who murdered them! They themselves used to drag people away and kill them and say that no one knows who murdered them. There was great fear.

18. I said to them, when I remembered this (the fear), I said, because of the horror, they said, I said: can't I come tomorrow during the day instead? They said: no, you have to come with us now! They said: the chief is waiting for you! You have to come now quickly!

19. So I said (to myself): what is there more than death? There is nothing worse than death, I said to myself, something, it is death! More than death there is nothing else!

20. So I dressed up and left with the police. I knocked on the chief's door; I arrived at the chief and knocked on his door. He came to me and said:

oh, come on in! He said so in a happy manner so to say, he showed me (respect).

21. He stood up and welcomed me and we sat down and talked. He said: it seems that because we did not have much, the chief said: because we did not have much contact, dialog with each other, this matter occurred, what you did. I said: I believe so, yes, it seems so. I do not know really, something like this.

22. He started, when we sat at his office, he started putting together a protocol about me, they call it *mazbata,* a protocol against me; why I said this and why I spoke in this way. So he started putting together a protocol about me and said, he asked, he asked and said: you, where are you from?

23. I said: we are the people, he asked about the Syriac people and said: where are you from? I said: we are the old people of Beth Nahrin, the old people of Mesopotamia. There are no other people older than us here. And our place is here.

24. He was annoyed when I said that. He did not like it when I said that our place is here and our “origin” is here.

25. When I noticed that he does not like what I am saying I said: if you do not believe me, come with me! We have a church, the church where I serve and where I live, it is two thousand years old, soon it will be two thousand years since it was build, which means that there was Syriac people here. And this church belongs to the Syriac people. Thus I said to him. He said: is that so? I said: yes, come with me and see for yourself!

26. So to continue, he took my identification card and wrote (my personal data) in the protocol. So, there I had said lots of things in the statement; whatever he asked I related for him.

27. I was held there. When it became midnight he was done with the protocol, the chief of security, he said: go over there and sit down. This is called “being watched”.

28. I went there and waited between the policemen. I waited until it became morning, awake between them and with them.

29. When it was one o’clock in the morning I asked if I could phone home to tell, to tell that I am safe and that it is nothing and do not, you do not have to worry about me.

30. They went and asked the chief and he said: alright. He continued: let him make a call. He went on: if not, the whole world will immediately

know about this, everyone will know that the priest is arrested and if they do not know.., what happened to him then they will get worry.

31. So he (one of the policemen) dialed, he said: tell me the number! I told him the number home and he dialed the number home, home to us. He said, when I spoke to my wife in Syriac, I spoke to my wife in Syriac, one of them hanged up the phone on me! He snatched it from my hand! He hanged up the phone on me! He said: what have you done?

32. I said: why do you do that for? I was goaded! Angry! But of course, they were policemen (and I could do not do much about it). So I was angry and said: why do you do this?

33. He said: in what language do you speak? I said: I speak in Syriac. And what do you say? I am telling them that I am ok and that they do not have to worry, I am calling home, my family. He said, he said, he got angry and said: why do you speak Syriac at home? How dare you speak Syriac at home?

34. I said: well, in what language should I speak? I said: I am a Syriac person. You came and dragged me from the church and indeed we speak Syriac at home and in Syriac we pray, we are Syriacs. I said: this is our language! I continued: this is an old language; there are no older languages than this. It is the language of Jesus.

35. He was very angry. He said: why do you speak Syr.., Syriac at home and did not speak, do not speak Turkish? I said: is that so? He said: yes! I said: I got angry and said: if you are, if you are, I said: a really tough guy, just look around you and see the whole of Diyarbakir, the whole of southeast (of Turkey) speaks Kurdish. Try to forbid them! Exactly these words I said to him!

36. Thus he too said, he was bewildered, he did not know what to say. He was silenced and did not know what to say. Then I went on and said: you obviously do not know, I was angry at him, I said: you do not know with who, how to handle, how to behave with (people), so to say, yes!

37. Thus I was there until the morning! And also the chief, and the chief in the morning, no, after that the policeman said: make your call! Make your call but speak in Turkish with your family!

38. He dialed the number, he dialed the number again and I spoke in Turkish with my family. I said, hm I said, I said, I said: now I will speak in Turkish with my wife it won't be … it is something very, how to say it, strange. She may not even recognize me and she may not talk to me either, I said.

39. He said: talk so that, so that we also know what you are saying and what you are doing, what hm.., at the end he dialed the number and I spoke in Turkish with my family. I said to them: I am good and there is nothing to worry about. Do not be concerned about me and so on.

40. After that I stayed there until the morning. At half past five in the morning, the chief came and said to me: get up! He said to me, he said: get up mister priest, when it was already morning! He said: get up! You have become famous. Thus he said to me.

41. Yeh sure, let it go, I said in anger. I was irritated. He said: get up and let two policemen take you home. I said: no! I was annoyed! I said: I am able to go home myself! He said: how are you going to go by yourself? I said: I will find a way. He said: no, no, let them follow you home.

42. They brought me home. We came home and it was five o'clock, closer to six in the morning. When I came home I thought of sleeping for a while. They did not let me sleep there! I thought of sleeping for a while. I slept for a while, about two hours. When it was eight o'clock they came and woke me up and said: come out, the policemen are here again they are asking about you. Now once again the policemen came to me.

43. I said to the policemen: what is it now? They said: you have to come with us, this time you are asked for by the, we call it here the prose.., the prosecutor, the regional public prosecutor office, prose.., the prosecutor, the highest position of the, in court here. The problem got obviously bigger and ... I said: so be it then.

44. So I left the policemen to go inside to get dressed and follow the policemen. The policemen asked me: have you not gone outside yet? I said: no, I have not gone out yet. I asked them: why do you ask? They said: well, the whole world's television networks and newspapers and so are here, just outside your door; they want to photograph you. I said: hm, let them then photograph, I do not care! The policemen said: no! They did not accept that! They did not let the journalists take photos of me.

45. Then, there were five of them, the policemen, civil, three of them went out and gathered the crowd of people and the newspaper and television people in one corner; they spoke to them in order to draw their attention while the other dragged me with them, escaping from there.

They took me somewhere else away from my church so that we came to the main road.[104]

46. They stopped a taxi, one of these yellow ones. They said: taxi driver stop! This man here, referring to me, is a condemned (criminal). They said to him: this one here is a convict. They told him this so that they will not have to pay him money for the ride.

47. They took me to the, what is it called, they took me to the court there. I went there and sat down and the policemen still with me. The district attorney that was in charge, this time, said: you will give the statement while standing!

48. I answered irritated and said: as you wish so it will be! I was annoyed! I was very distressed and said to myself: whatever happens I do not care and whatever comes to my mind I will say it without thinking of the consequences.

49. Thus he started reading up the whole statement that I gave in the evening, in the night. He reads up all that statement and says: have you given this statement? I said: yes, I gave it. He asked: do you have anything else to add to it? I answered: yes. There is something more to add to it!

50. So at that time they had written about me in the newspapers, here in Turkey "the traitor among us" and there was also the cross in my hand, in my … they had obviously seen it. You may also have seen in the … "the traitor among us"! They made all this up so that someone will come and kill me! See all this was thought through!

51. They wrote "the traitor among us"! Do you understand? They are all Muslims and I am the only Christian and priest! I acknowledged the kil.., the massacre, the ethnical cleansing of the Armenian and the Syriac people. I said: I am saying that the massacre occurred and I admit it took place!

52. Consequently, for the reason that someone will come and murder me, they made up all this, they presented the matter in this way. So he read up, he read up the statement, this distr.., he read up the whole statement that I had given. He asked: do you have something more to add? I answered: yes! I said: they are presenting me as a traitor there (in the newspapers)!

---

104 Keep in mind that the church lies in a quarter in Diyarbakir with narrow alleys and paths where no one can move around anonymously.

53. I said: we are Syriac people. I continued: we have been living here for thousands of years and also within the state of Turkey, since long time back, since long centuries back in time we are living side by side with the state. And we are good people to this state.

54. But the state, the state of Turkey does not know our ... did not appreciate our significance, I mean the state did not know the value of us being fine people, being what is it called, that we had a culture, that we had something particu.., did not appreciate our value. I said: we serve in the military, we pay taxes, we ... whatever is asked from us, what is needed from us, we offer it to the state.

55. But they are presenting me as a "traitor" here, they write that I am a "traitor"! I would like you to write down there that the one who is calling me a "traitor", the traitor must be he himself! So actually the district attorney wrote down this too, he added it to my statement and ... Thereafter the district attorney ordered two policemen to bring me home again. After that I was sent to the district court proceedings.

56. At court they pleaded for six, from four to six years in jail. The charge is known as three hundred twelve, 312! It means that when someone tries to split the people, as if I would divide the people, for example as if I would split the Syriac people and make them rise up against the state of Turkey, something like this.

57. Three hundred, the case is known as three hundred twelve. They sentenced me to jail four to six years, they pleaded for this sentence, as I mentioned. So they sent me to district court proceedings.

58. At the court hearings, as you know, lots of people came to the court; people came from Sweden and also from, from Germany came people and there were people, there were, there were between them some people from the parliament of Sweden and there were people from the human rights organizations, in Syriac we say *zədqe nušoye* and from the Europ.., European Union also.

59. And at that time also the ambassador of Germany,[105] he also had written a letter for me and sent it with the delegation. He sent me a letter saying that he sends me greetings and wishing me what is it called ... this kind of words he wrote in his letter.

60. And they (the delegations) came with me all the way to the court, to the first court hearings. And this showed, of course a huge demonst..,

105 In the text father Akbulut says *ǧumhūr bašqāni* "president" which is not very likely. For this reas I chose to translate it to "ambassador".

as you would say a huge support. It was obvious that Turkey was afraid then. All these came to the court hearings with me! When I attended the hearings.

61. The judge started reading that article in the newspaper of Hurriyat, where I was photographed with a cross in my hand. He said: did you, he addressed the question to me while all the people that had come (from out of the country) had entered the court hall; these ones were almost forty, maybe fifty people, he said, he said: I will now read, have you made all these statements? He started then reading the article in Hurriyat. I said: yes, we talked about this, I said these things and the journalist put them there, he wrote them there (in the newspaper).

62. Thus, after that they postponed the court hearings, after noticing that a large group of people came from Europe to attend the hearings, they postponed it. And also the second time, also, also they called me to the court hearings. Once again, my lawyers, I mean, they presented what had to be presented and they did not … I also said what was needed to be said, I mean, I did not withdraw my statement, I did not deny what I said before.

63. The third date for the court hearings, was like the two before it. This was all due to the crowds of our people who were engaged in this case. Many were engaged and showed immense courage. Everyone of our people in Europe showed immense courage. As you may know, in Germany there were maybe five, six thousand people that went on hunger strike for a day to express their opinion against Turkey.

64. All these facts were brought, were brought forward to the, to the judge here. See here, this is how the case is; the whole people are following up this case and supporting the priest and there is no way out.

65. So they were scared and that is why they did not sentence me. Another thing, fact may be that, that as I understood it, that also the consul, the consul of the United States had asked me, of the United States had asked me saying: did they torture you? Did they insult you?

66. I said: no, they did not torture me but because I spok.., because I am speaking Syriac at home one of them was displeased with me. He was furious! He said to me: Why do you speak Syriac at home? All these aspects I had presented them to the consul also.

67. And of course there were among our people those who were scared, for example those living in Istanbul, the Merdellis.[106] They were very, very

106 Merdellis originate from the famous Mardin.

scared and asked me to deny what I stated. They said, they said: take it back and deny what you have said, deny it in the ne.., in the newspapers and on television.

68. I said: no, I will not deny and cannot do that. And I had also said, as you know, in the newspapers, the first time this case appeared there, that I am a priest and do not lie and it does not suit me to lie. This whole matter is true and it happened and this is what I said there, in the newspapers and hence I will never take it back and deny it. Thus I said to them.

69. And there were some of our people that were very, that were very afraid, those who are wealthy, that are such. There was this one who said to me, he called me and said on the phone: you have burned us up, you have burned us up, these were his exact words, you have burned us up! How can you do something like this?

70. I said to him: is that so? What have I done to burn you up? He said: you cannot make this kind of announcement. I said: I have already said it and it is done; I said: I have already said it and it is done. What I have said, I said it and it is done and will not come back, thus I told him.

71. Well, he said, he said: I will send the television (journalist) to you and you will say, you withdraw the whole matter and so. I said: I cannot do such a thing. What I stated is true! My conscience is calm and I just spoke the truth and that is all.

72. And this way it was. Our people in general showed great, what is it called, against … But I have to say that I always thank our people for their support to me in this case. I thank them all for the great courage they showed in this matter.

73. This whole issue had taken on huge proportions from the beginning. As I mentioned, as I said, it was also broadcast on television; this was clearly not only my case but the case of all the Syriac people, our people, all Christians!

74. When the massacres started the murderers did not think that we will only slaughter these or those. They slaughtered whole groups people, anyone that came in their way, the whole Christian population. If the murderers had a chance they would have finished them totally.

75. Nevertheless, this may be, as we say, something divine. When the judge asked me; I still cannot believe how some of the people asked me to take back what I said, when the judge asked me and said, said … I had a flashback, everything (the horror of the massacre that I heard about)

came back to me again and I thought to myself: how can I say this never happened, my conscience did not accept it, it did not allow it.

76. I said to myself: so many many people they slaughtered, so much killing, they slaughtered priests, bishops, monks and did not show any kind of mercy towards them. How can I say that this never occurred? I said, I said: this took place for sure and I am not afraid of the consequences of what I am saying.

77. Could the consequences be harder that death? What they did to us can never be undone again. Thus I thought: what they have done to us is already done and they cannot do more than tha. I thought: if they want to do more, so be it then. But what they already have done it is done. It happened and it is true.

78. And this is, as you may have heard, this case was known all over the world. I had also stated in the newspapers, that I will make my voice heard all over the world and we are, we are demanding our rights. Why were we without any reason or guilt massacred? Why did they put, bring a Sayfo over us. Exactly this way I was thinking at that time.

79. Many people, I do not wish to name names here, pleaded with me to withdraw what I said. Among them also priests, other people; they said: they will murder you! Some of them said, they said: they will kill you and close down the church.

80. I answered and said: let them then kill me! I am in no way better than all those that were massacred! Let them close down the church! If the church will be closed down because of me, let them then kill … close it down! The church cannot … it won't be that easy to close down the church. So, this is it, this is how it is.

81. Three times I was examined in the highest court in Diyarbakir in Turkey. Three times just because I said that the Syriac people were massacred, a Sayfo was brought over them. That is all.

5. Text 2

1. *bə-šṛolo es.., e, hiya i=ṣbuṯo, ṣbuṯo rapṯo hawyo-wa bə-šṛolo, hawyo aʿmi. ono-ste yaʿni naqqat kmiʿağabno; komaṇṇo: məš=šəkəl xaləṣno mina.*

2. *hiye, i=naqqa d-.., i=naqqa d-əḥkəmno bat=.., komaṇṇo tlaṯmo w ḥḏaḥṣar, i=dăʿwa d-ətlaṯmo w ḥḏaḥṣar. harke b-Turkya d-əmmina ḥa d-foləġ u=ʿamo, yaʿni d-maqəmle ʿal i=dawla.*

3. *maʿnata*[107] *eli fləġli as= səryoye, maqimili ʿal i=dawla t-Turkya. mu=.., mu=.., mu=xṣuṣan..,*[108] *yaʿni mu=medano ḥkəmno u tlaṯ kore, tlaṯ kore ḥkəmno bi=maḥkăma ʿelayto, yaʿni d-kəmminala ʿelayto, i=rapṯo t-arke, d-Dyarbakər, d-Turkya.*

4. *w at=tlaṯ kore-sti, halbat*[109] *xut kətyo iḏiʿo alxu, aṯi, aṯi noše folitiqore, noše d-əmmina, noše b-darġe ʿeloye, du=Swed, xəd qonṣoloṣe aṯi, dəṯxu hayo i=wazərto barayto aṯyowa. hayo d-əqṭilalle.*

5. *tlaṯ kore aṯyo, aṯənwa xut-tani noše rabe, b-darġe ʿeloye aṯənwa. aṯənwa li=maḥkămayḏi w, u xaləṣno mina .., küḏʿat, hiye harke, harke mu=.., mi=dăʿwaṯe, tlaṯmo ḥḏaḥṣar, noše harke-ste ḥkim, d-əmmina b-Turk.., b-gawe=t-Turkya, d-kə́twayne, d-əmmina xŭd d-ŭʿdo diḏan, u=riš waziro diḏan. ʿayni*[110] *dăʿwa ḥkim.*

6. *hiye tre xabre, d-latwayne diḏe, d-ḥa, tre kaṯowe-wayne, ḥkim w xile ḥăpəs, daməx ḥăpəs w hule zuze. bass ono xaləṣno mina. halbat haṯe, haṯe lo hawxa mede fšiqo hawyo. p-aṯe halbat gmaškaṇṇo u=ʿamayḏan kule, yaʿni u=ʿamayḏan kule d-hawili mʿadrono w əmsaʿdono d-maqəmme d-əmmina orifi li=raġlo.*

7. *kito hənn t-səmme halxe, kito hənn t-ṣayimiwa, kətwa hənn d-ġălăbe t-səmwalle ḥṭufye lağ.., ḥfiṭoṯo lăğani. p-awxa, p-awxa, p-awxa xaləṣno aṣāṣ. maškaṇṇo u=ʿamayḏan ġălăbe w …*

8. *w halbat i=măsăle măsăle rapṯo-wa, xəd məḻḻi. maʿnata, maʿnata ono i=naqqa d-əḥkəmno d-lo-.., d-lo-maḥətlali*[111] *bu=ḥăpəs; hiya ṭəlbowayli ḥăpəs u kito xŭd məḻḻi bu=šəklayḏi d-əḥkimi ġălăbe noše harke-sti, damixi ḥăpəs maʿnata maqbela yaʿni, i=ṣbuṯo du=sayfo d-hawi ʿal u=ʿamayḏan.*

---

107 Cf. Ara. *maʿna* “meaning”.
108 Cf. Tur. *husus* “matter, question; particular”.
109 Cf. Kur. *helbet* “certainly, of course”.
110 Cf. Tur. *aynı* “the same, equal, identical”.
111 It is referred to the court here, as feminine.

9. *u bə-šṛolo, yaʿni, yaʿni mu=yawmo, yaʿni ono mu=yawmo d-koḏaʿno ruḥi koḏaʿno d-hawi, hawi u=sayfano ʿal u=ʿamayḏan. bass maʿ əl-ʾăsaf,*[112] *kito mu=ʿamayḏan, mu=ʿamayḏan yaʿni kito d-hēš lo=komaqbli d-hawi sayfo. hēš yaʿni d-kəmmi lawi.*

10. *ono gabi u=ḥa d-lo maqbəl hawi sayfo maʿnata, maʿnata xayə.., hani komәḥšowi, xəd, məš=šəkəl d-omaṇṇŭx, ḥa d-oməṛ xayin latyo šafiro, elo mede hawxa. e, ánnaqla balki-stene hənnək-sti koṭəʿni, d-əmmina ġamo d-lo=we mede. ya gzayʿi. ya … yaʿni ḥa kibe d-oballe ḥaqq-sti*[113] *naqqawat.*

11. *ama*[114] *bass ḥa lə=glozəm zoyəʿ. haṯi i=šṛolo-yo. hano, hano u=makṯab zabnayḏan-yo, u=tarixayḏan-yo.*[115] *layban kŭfrina ebe-ste. aḥna xəd əmšiḥoye, hăka qṭilina ʿal foṯe=t-kә́twayna mšiḥoye, ʿal foṯe=d-mšiḥo, layban kŭfrina. lo=lazəm kŭfrina eba-sti, fahimat?*

12. *e hawxayo, halbat bəṯər mi=ṣbuṯayo d-xaləṣno mina, maškərina Aḷoho d-xaləṣno mina d-lo hno, d-lo zə.., d-lo tahlŭkat*[116] *d-lo mede, d-lo zəḥṯo. hawi xaliṣina maškərina Aḷoho.*

13. *bəṯər mina hawi, howe-wa măsălat d-əmmina. kətwa d-əmmina naqlawat ḥa, u=ʿamo t-kətwa t-tarke, u=waxtawo halbat, yaʿni ŭʿdo hani košapəʿ aʿla balki taqriban*[117] *traḥṣar=əšne mede. i=naqlayo ḥayriwa, kətwa b-ʿayno lo ṭawto ebi. d-əmmina d-ḥayriwa ebi harke ġălăbe.*

14. *balki ḥzalxu, šamiʿutu, u=ḥa, a=ʿlayme d-əzzənwa w duʿṛiwa, u=ʿamo moḥənwa rapsat bat=tarʿayḏan w ba=.., w ba=.., w əmmiwaylan xabre. u kətwa d-əmmina moḥənwa kefe-sti me, me lalʿal, mu=šuṛo di=ʿito, moḥənwa kefe eban u ṭawriwa d-əmmina ğamāt.*[118] *w saymiwa ġălăbe hno, həṣrono aʿlayna bam=medonani, u=waxtawo halbat. ŭʿdo ṭaw-tər-yo.*

15. *bəṯər kibi d-omaṇṇo ʿal lawxa-sti, naqqa măsăla, kibi d-obeno ṭofṣo, naqqa kətwo hən naʿime, ʿlayme, d-əmmina arbaḥṣar ḥamšaḥṣar=əšne, w d-rabtər-sti, moḥənwa kefe.*

16. *naqqa azzí nafəqno məḷḷi l-ḥa, omaṇṇo: qay gmoḥat kefe, yaʿni hawxa eban aḥna? məs=səmlan ebŭx? məḷḷi la.., lan=nošayḏe hīč lo=hnalle ebi. yaʿni hawxa lo=ḥəṛṛe b-.., hīč lə=uwwalli foṯo, hawxa xəd ḥa d-əmmi: hat ḥaqq-hat; kmaliqat d-moḥən kefe ebŭx yaʿni.*

112 Cf. Tur. *maalesef* "unfortunately".
113 Cf. Tur. *hak* "right, true".
114 Cf. Tur. *ama* "but, yet, still".
115 Cf. Tur. *tarih* "history".
116 Cf. Tur. *tehlike* "danger".
117 Cf. Ara. *taqriban* "approximately, almost".
118 Cf. Tur. *cam* "glass, window".

17. *e, w naqqat-sti disa ḥa, ḥa naʿimo mḥewo disa kefe. disa, disa azzí məḷḷi la=.., yaʿni ḥoziwaynanne harke, ḥeḏorayna taqriban kŭḏʿinanne, me zabno yarixo ono harke, azzí mə…, məḷḷi lu=babo. u=babo m.., məṛle: zŭx marke! hawxa, hawxa lo ṭawwo, b-naxwaš,*[119] *hawxa hno, məṛle: zŭx marke! xəd dəmmat yaʿni məqšat, hawxa mede. edi ṭreli mine halbat, hedi.*

18. *b-ḥa may=yawme-sti, b-ḥa yawmo-sti kətwo ḥa disa m.., ʿlaymo rab.., yaʿni kəpwayle ḥamšaḥṣar əštaḥṣar=əšne. hawxa mazʿaqle bəṯri oməṛ yaʿni: "păpāz păpāz", yaʿni qašo qašo. hawxa mqašmaḷḷe*[120] *aʿli.*

19. *məḷḷi: d-man-hat? məḷḷi: ma, hayko-yo u=baytayḏŭx? azzé mahzamle. aḥ=ḥawrone mə́ṛṛali: zŭx, kalé u=baytaḏe harke. azzí məḷḷi, omaṇṇo: u=abraṯxu hawxa koməṛ. ha.., hanək-sti, yaʿni xəd dəmmat, xəd dəmmat lo b-ʿayno hno, yaʿni xəd lo=ḥaruwwe, xəd dəmmat med.., ṭawwo səmle ebŭx yaʿni hawxa.*

20. *hawxa bu=šəklano ha.., howewo medone aʿmayna bə-šṛolo. u=ḥa yawmo-sti kə́twaylan d-əmmina naqla hawxa ḏayfe,*[121] *orḥe bi=dərto yatiwayna. ḥzelŭx i=dərtayḏan. bu=qayṭo koyətwina tamo. mḥalle kefe nafiqina, qəm ʿasṛiyye. nafiqina kalə́n, be man, kḥozina man komoḥe koḥozina qay komoḥən.*

21. *ḥəḷḷan kalə́n kəppe, kəppe balki ʿasṛo ḥamšaḥṣar ʿlayme, ḥaṭroṯe, skine măsălat b-iḏayye. lo=.., yaʿni lo=mağrelan d-əmqadmina-sti. lə=mqadamlan, d-əmmina d-nofəq mede mina. kə́twaylan ḏayfe-sti yatiwe mʿağbi. fayiši hawxa ʿəğbo,*[122] *kəmmi: áydarbo kowe hawxa medone, ḏayfe yatiwe.*

22. *u xət hawxa medone, hawxa, aḥan fayəš yaʿni yalifiwayna, xəd d-əmmat hawiwa normal*[123] *elan. yaʿni kŭl=gave d-əmmina gnəfqatwa gdəmmiwalŭx xabro; gdəmmiwalŭx păpāz păpāz, gawər*[124] *gawər, yaʿni. gawər yaʿni maʿnayḏa lo=komətyaqnat la-Aḷoho, e hawxa.*

23. *hawxa medone hawxa ġălăbe əmmiwa bəṯrayna w b-ḥa.., w moḥənwa kefe eban w moḥənwa kefe ʿəl mi=.., əh, ʿəl mi=.., ʿəl mu=šuṛo di=ʿito-da*[125] *eban. xəd məḷḷi ṭawriwa ağ=ğamatayḏan, ṭawriwa medone. saymiwa ḥəṣrono li=ʿito w elan tavda.*[126] *w bu=tarʿo moḥənwa.*

---

119 Cf. Kur. *nexweş* "bad, ill, sick".
120 Cf. Tur. *kaşmer* "clown, fool, buffoon".
121 Cf. Ara. *ḍayf* "guest, visitor".
122 Cf. Ara. *uʿǧūba* "strange, wonder, unheard-of thing".
123 Cf. Tur. *normal* "normal".
124 Cf. Tur. *gâvur* "non-Muslim, infidel, unbeliever".
125 Cf. Tur. adverb *de/da* "also, too".
126 Cf. Kur. *tevde* "together".

24. *w kətwa d-əmmina ġălăbe maṭ=ṭaye-sti t-harke aṣāṣ, yaʿni bu=šəršaṯṯe, hēš mu=sayfo d-omaṇṇo, məštawtfe, mu=sayfo, ġălăbe mənne, yaʿni maǧ=ǧəddaṯe w ma=.., mar=rabaṯṯe, hawen, d-əmmina u=waxtawo hawen ṭaye žboyəd lo=qəṭlənne.*

25. *ánnaqa hani an=.., an=naḏ.., an=nobġaṯṯe, an=navikaṯṯe,*[127] *an=nobġaṯṯe d-əmmina, d-əʿdo d-kofayši, ġălăbe mənne-sti, kətwa hən mənne-sti d-əmmina məfṣoḥiwa bu=medano. ḥatta aṯi hən, d-əmmina gabi, xəd dəmmat mtabrəkili*[128] *yaʿni, d-əmmi, d-əmmi ṭawwo səmlŭx. d-əmmi ṭawwo səmlŭx. ma mə=ksaymi ebŭx?*

26. *hani u=šəršaṯṯe mšiḥoye-ne. kīt harke ġălăbe mənne. d-əmmat ma qay lo=kowən mšiḥoye? lo=kowən, xliṭi bə-ḥḏoḏe. d-əmmina kito ġălăbe. ŭʿdo kibŭx d-əmmat bam=mo ḥamši balki, haymen, u=ḥa d-əmšaylat mene, u=šəršayḏe mšiḥoyo-yo. yaʿni mu=waxt du=sayfo, yaʿni d-lo məqṭoli qana.*

27. *w ġălăbe komaḥkəlli măsal,*[129] *kibi d-obenŭx ṣbuṯo ʿal lawxa. d-ommanŭx mede ʿal lawxa-sti. naqqa aṯi ḥa gabi. d-əmmina kəppwele qaḏar əšti=šne-wa hiye. aṯi mə́ḷḷeli: ḥoli hat-at.*

28. *omaṇṇo: məš=šəkəl kowe? oməṛ: ḥoli-hat. áydarbo? oməṛ: emi mənxo-yo. e məš=šəkəl? oməṛ, oməṛ: naqqa səmme d-əmmina, i=naqqayo əmmiwayla qafle, yaʿni saymiwanne qaflāt an=noše, yaʿni gəroḅāt,*[130] *fahimat? kofəhmat?*

29. *oməṛ: saymiwanne gəroḅāt u məbliwayne qəṭliwayne w ḍuʿriwa. d-əmmina, oməṛ: emi-sti naqqa mballe qafle; hano u=ṭayo komaḥkeli, koməṛ: emi baynoṯayye-wa. emi mənxo-wa. baynoṯayye-wa. hiya-sti ḥḏo manək d-mitawbilowa lu=qatlo-wa. məblənne, oməṛ: kətwa, kətwa ḥḏo pire baynoṯayye b-at.., ṭʿənto balki tmənyo yarḥe.*

30. *oməṛ: at=tranək d-məblənne səmme mqarrasiyye, mǧadala*[131] *hawxa ʿam əḥḏoḏe. ḥa məṛle: naʿimo-yo w ḥa məṛle: kaččəke-yo,*[132] *barṯo-yo, ḥa məṛle: abro-yo. hawxa səmme mqarrası hul dl-ayko, ml=ḥuruyto madle i-xanğar čəṛṛe gawa, di=.., di=pire, di=pire mofaqle u=naʿimo oməṛ məṛle: ḥzay be naʿimo-yo kaččəke-yo, yaʿni?*

31. *yaʿni hawxa hŭl i=dărăǧayo aṭ=ṭaye t-arke komaḥkən. yaʿni hano=medano maḥkeleli u=medano, u=ṭayo, w xŭt-tanṯe ġălăbe măsayl koṯən yaʿni*

---

127 Cf. Kur. *nevî* "grandchild".
128 Cf. Tur. *tebrik* "congratulation, congratulating".
129 Cf. Tur. *misal* "example".
130 Cf. Tur. *grup* "group".
131 Cf. Tur. *cedel* "dispute, wrangle".
132 Cf. Kur. *keç* "girl, daughter".

gmәğġoli aˁmi. kīt hani t-kәnne hawxa bu=šәklano d-әmmina ġălăbe gruḥmilan. kәmmi: hatu ṭawwe-hatu; ṭaw minan-hatu. hәnnәk kәmmi yaˁni.

32. *w bu=šәklano kito ġălăbe mәnne d-kәnne, d-әmmina xәd mәḻḻi bu=šәršo mšiḥoye w, u hawxa. w d-әmmina kәtwa ḥa-sti i=naqqa, i=naqqa d-nafәqno waxt, i=naqqa d-hawyo i=măsăle, elo hәnnәk-sti, d-әmmina hәnnәk w hani a=hno lә=kṯәn l-ḥḏoḏe, i=qŭṭnuṯo d-Turkya, lә=kṯәn. lanne basime.*

33. *ánnaqa hani d-kәnne minan, naqqa nafәqno, măsal aṯi ḥa bu=tarˁo aṯi nšәqle bayne=ˁayni, hawxa msawyo; ḥa zlām*[133] *hawxa rabo-wa bu=ˁumro. kibe šawˁi=šne taqriban yaˁni. aṯi nšәqle bayne=ˁayni omәṛ: at=tarte ˁayne-hat. omәṛ: ṭawwo sәmlŭx, yaˁni hawxa húwleli moral.*[134]

34. *omәṛ: ṭawwo sәmlŭx. omәṛ: mә-ksaymi? omәṛ: tro=ṯәn mšayli mini, ono-sti gdommano d-hawi sayfo w aḥna, w aḥna ab=.., ar=rabayḏan, aq=qamoyayḏan mšiḥoye-wayne. hŭl d-hawo, hŭl u=ṭayo hawxa d-máṛḻeli, u ġălăbe. w hēš kŭl=d-әkḥozeli, kḥozeno naqqat, hēš d-әkmaḥwe ˁălaqa*[135] *basәmto ġălăbe aˁmi, esore basime.*

35. *kito bu=šәklano-sti u kәtwa hawxa-sti. ánnaqa әˁdo i=aġlab, bam=mo, bam=mo yaˁni tәšˁi, kibŭx d-әmmat, tmoni tәšˁi mbadli d-әmmina. hәnnәk mbadli ˁam әḥḏoḏe u, mbadli yaˁni aˁmayna, ˁam a=mšiḥoye-sti.*

36. *fayәš ab=baladiyyat*[136] *d-әmmina eli kәtli esore ˁmayye. w ḥatta ono-sti bi=baladiyye kito, kito kәmminale maġlis*[137] *dann=arbˁi suhḏe ono-sti bu=maġlisawo-no. yaˁni kmaydi i=fәkrayḏi-sti, i=baladiyye hŭl әˁdo. әˁdo aṯilan baladiyye ḥaṯo garak*[138] *ˁayni hawxa d-.., d-әmhalxi, bu=šәklano.*

37. *mәd-kowe medone kәmšawri eban, măsăla saymina hawxa ṭawwo-yo saymina, ḥatta maqәmlan qoyәmto harke, yaˁni ˁ-laˁ=ˁame d-әẓlimi*[139] *harke, harke bi=baladiyye, ˁam әḥḏoḏe. ˁ-laˁ=ˁame d-әẓlimi, yaˁni d-әḥzalle ˁazquṯo ġălăbe harke. lo=kәmmi ftiḥo ˁal u=sayfo.*

38. *hәnnәk lo=kәmmi hawxa. bass kәmmi: ˁ-laˁ=aˁame d-әẓlimi. kṯәwwe aˁla bu=sәryoyo, bu=tәrki, bu=armnoyo, bu=kәrdi w bu=.., u b-lešone hawxa kṯәwwe ˁal i=qoyәmtayo. w hl-i=dărăğayo yaˁni hawxa mḥalfi.*

39. *aḥna, ono kәtli d-әmmina esore ġălăbe ṭawwe ˁmayye. halbat lo ba=.., bam=mo mo mḥalfi, bam=mo kibŭx d-әmmat tmoni, d-әmḥalәf u=ˁamo t-arke. w, w kәtlan esore ṭawwe ˁmayye w xәt hawxa măsayәl d-әmmina.*

---

133 Cf. Kur. *zelam* "man".
134 Cf. Tur. *moral* "courage, support".
135 Cf. Tur. *alaka* "connections, tie, relationship".
136 Cf. Tur. *belediye* "municipality".
137 Cf. Tur. *meclis* "assembly, council, board".
138 Cf. Kur. *gerek* "necessary, must".
139 Cf. Tur. *zulüm* "injustice, oppression, tyranny".

aḥna, aḥna, aḥna u=ʿamo t-arke, diḏan as=səryoye d-əmmina hēš, yaʿni hēš hawxa hne-ne ġălăbe latte hāž[140] *lo m.., kito mənne mənne latte hāž lo=d-hawi sayfo w lo lo.*

40. *w latte, u lo=kəbʿi máqəbli, kito hawxa šəklat-sti baynoṯayna-sti. yaʿni aḥna glozam u=ʿamo suryoyo kulan howina ʿayni bu=fəkrano d-.., aḥna d-hawi sayfo ʿlayna. aḥna i=naqqa d-əqṭilina lo hən minan qṭil w ṭralle hən. əbʿi d-qŭṭli kŭlle, u=ʿamayḏan kule.*

41. *ʿal l-awxa kulan glozəm d-howina bu=.., bu=fəkrano ḥiṣe ʿam əḥḏoḏe, mḥayḏe ʿam əḥḏoḏe. u i=ṣbuṭaṭe yaʿni xəd əḥzelŭx bi=ṣbuṭayo diḏi, du=sayfo d-əšmiʿo ġălăbe, šmiʿowa, lazəm kŭl=ḥa minan d-əmğahəd yaʿni bu=šəklano. d-əmmət hawi, d-hawi u=medano aʿlayna, aḥna qṭilina. liʾən.., čunku*[141] *i=dŭkṯayḏan kula fayišo harke.*

42. *d-əmmina u=ʿamayḏan d-kə́twaylan, aḥna kətlan makṯab zabno harke ʿatiqo. kətlan d-əmmina ʿamo ʿatiqo. kətla kŭltūr ʿatiqo. kətlan lešono ʿatiqo, aʿtaq mene d-layto harke bi=dŭkṯaṯe. əšma di=dŭkṯaṯe-sti aḥna, elan hulan yaʿni. haṯe ydəḥto-yo*[142] *yaʿni, əšma di=ğoġraf.., di=ğoġrafiyaṯe*[143] *kula, d-əmmina d-Beṯ Nahrin, w əd-gawa kule.*

43. *aḥna maḥətlan aʾ=ʾəšmonani, hani. w əyḏiʿo-yo, i=naqqa d-əmmət əšma=di=dŭkṯo b-səryoyo-yo, bu=.., bu=lešonaḏan-yo. ʿal l-awxa ḥna, aḥna lazəm bu=šəklano mətfakrina, bu=šəklano ḥayṣina ḥḏoḏe, bu=šəklano miḥayḏina, w b-hawxa.*

44. *w aḥna, aḥna, yaʿni haṯe bam=mo mo-yo. layto, layto ʾabadan hno eba d-.., d-hawi sayfo ʿlayna. w ḥatta naqqa hawi-wa harke, əʿdo mə=t-kowe ẓatan*[144] *ono kəḏʿili d-əmmina xd as=sniġre xəttayna d-kənne noše hne hēš, ayna t-ḥozəlli kəḏʿili kəmmi, i=naqla t-kowe măsayəl t-kəbʿina d-əmmina, d-.., t-kəbʿi məğġanno ʿmayye bat=tălăfəzyōne aw b-medone. kŭḏʿi. komanṇane.*

45. *kŭḏʿi yaʿni, i=naqqa t-kuḏʿi ono d-mərlwayli, yaʿni xəl hawino xət t əmmat sambol*[145] *t-hawxa du=sayfo. naqqawat kəmmi, kommanṇo: yawo*[146] *kŭl=gave lo=quḍrina, ḥa, ḥa ku.., kuhne harke b-.., mu=ʿamayḏan gzoyəʿ, lo mi=dawla. ánnaqa ṭray, mu=ʿamayḏan ḥa kozoyəʿ.*

---

140 Cf. Kur. *haj* "awareness, information".
141 Cf. Tur. *çünkü* "because".
142 Regressive divoicing of ʿ to *ḥ*.
143 Cf. Tur. *coğrafya* "geography".
144 Cf. Tur. *zaten* "in any case, as a matter of fact".
145 Cf. Tur. *sembol* "symbol".
146 Cf. Tur. *yahu* "see here! look here!".

46. *ono d-lo disa gdomaṇṇo. yaʿni disa kibi məğġanno, samno raportaže*[147] *disa. ánnaqa m-awxa küḏʿili. xəd hawino d-əmmat sambol du=sayfo yaʿni. külle küḏ.., iḏiʿo-yo yaʿni lu=ʿamayḏan-sti w l-ayna d-.., laq=qaroyo, d-əmmina laq=qaroye, las=sniġre, la=.., la=.., lan=nahire du=ʿamo, t-arki-sti w diḏan-sti.*

47. *hawxa, w t-owelüx šuwole mede? yaʿni bə-šṛolo məqqa d-ommano yaʿni gdəmmat balki kuhne ruḥe, hano yaʿni šəbhoro-yo lo eli w bass; küḏʿat ono máṛṛali əmmi: dʿaṛ eba! dʿaṛ eba! yaʿni u=ʿamo t-arke, diḏan, dʿaṛ eba gqüṭlilüx, čaykilüx*[148] *bu=ḥăpəs.*

48. *omaṇṇo: lanno lo ṭaw m-ani d-əqṭili ʿal awxa, lanno ṭaww me ḥa mənne. w ġălăbe maḥətte b-.., qṭilənne w baḥ=ḥbušye w bah=hne. ono-sti ṭr=oweno tabaʿ t-anək omaṇṇo. yaʿni hawxa mətfakaḷḷi. w báṯərke mede šṛolo-wa.*

49. *i=naqqa d-duʿṛat b-mede hano ebe makṯab zabno-yo, yaʿni bə-qḏoli kfoyašwa, eli mede lo ṭawwo l-ağani. bəṯər kfoyašwa mede lo ṭawwo eli. bass əʿdo d-əmmina məḷḷi, xəd məḷḷi bu=šawṭo, hawi ṭawwo eli, lu=ʿamayḏan qamayto. eli, ma ono xlo məḷḷüx ono, yaʿni lu=ʿamo, lu=sayfo hawi mede hno ṭawwo d-əmmina.*

50. *d-əmmina kibe waxt t-oṯe d-how mede kibe d-əmmi ma qay ḥa šab.., bə-flān*[149] *zabno, flān qašo, qašo Yusef məṛle: hawi sayfo w kalé ha.., lawi mede. ḥa ánnaqa koməftəḥ u=tarʿo hedi*[150] *hedi xəd dəmmat.*

51. *u ġălăbe dăʿwat, d-əmmina bi=dăʿwaṯe d-xaləṣno mina, harke b-Turkya, ġălăbe dăʿwat hawyo d-əmmina zbəṭla d-əmmina bahro, l-dăʿwat hēš, yaʿni maḥkămat hēš əd-ʿame hēš, d-noše hēš yaʿni. măsăla kəppe d-əmmi qay, ma bə-flān dăʿwa kalé ḥkim bam=maḥkămat.*

52. *ann=avoqate*[151] *kəppe d-əmmi ḥkim flān kass, flān qašo lo=čəkke bu=ḥaps, măsăla. haṯe d-əmmat ṭəfṣo, örnak*[152] *yaʿni, kuyo yaʿni l-ġălăbe medone, gẓubṭo bahro l-medone hēš, l-dăʿwat hēš.*

53. *yaʿni máṛṛali: dʿaṛ! məqqa d-məṛṛe-sti ono lo=maḥətli b-hawni d-doʿaṇṇo. yaʿni ono bi=maḥkăma mətyaqán mətfakarli omaṇṇo: haqqa aḥna, ono bi=qriṯayḏi d-əmmina tre yarḥe kamile mḥarabbe b-ʿIwardo.*

---

147 Cf. Tur. *röportaj* "report".
148 Cf. Kur. *çek* "to put in".
149 Cf. Tur. *filan* "so-and-so, a certain person".
150 Cf. Ara. *hādiʾ* "calm, quiet", occurs normally *hedi hedi* "slowly".
151 Cf. Tur. *avukat* "lawyer".
152 Cf. Tur. *örnek* "example". The priest seems some times to level his vocabulary to my own since he knows my background as an academic person and as a speaker of also Arabic besides Turoyo, e.g.: the use of words such as *ṭəfṣo, măsal* (text 2:33) and *örnek* in the same meaning.

54. *yaʿni hēš kofayši ag=garme, ag=garme t-kofayši kalə́n ba=dkotanək. hēš kalə́n ab=buġre du=silāḥ*[153] *bi=ʿito, b-maṛ Ḥušabo, i=ʿitaydan. hēš hŭl l-əʿdo kfayši. u, i=yemo, u bə́ṯərke ono, ono naʿimo i=yemo d-babi ḥzéwayla u=sayfo. naqqawat kmaḥwəlla bu=tălăfəziōn-sti. maḥənwayla naqqawat.*

55. *hiya ṭəʿnowa buġre, d-əmmina mʿawnowa. hiya ḥzela u=sayfo kŭl=gave maḥkyowaylan d-əmmina. maḥkyowa. w qrelan-sti, lo hiya d-maḥkyo, qrelan ba=kṯowe w qrelan ma u=waxtano. bass hiya maḥkelalan ġălăbe ḥna naʿime. hēš čučəkāt*[154] *koṯe l-bolan d-əmmina.*

56. *ŭʿdo mḥasyo halbat d-, hani kibe šēṯ, šwaʿ=əšne. u hiya maḥkyowaylan am=medone d-howenwa. w d-əmmina ġălăbe harke ŭʿdo, xəd məḻḻi ġălăbe kito harke ṣəbwoṯo, kšəmʿina maṭ=ṭaye. hənnək kəmmi, yaʿni hənnək.*

57. *aḥna kyətwina naqqawat ʿam i=baladiyye, di=baladiyye, u=rayis*[155] *di=baladiyye, naqqa, lo mə́ḻḻilŭx koweno ono bu=maǧlis ono-sti, kyətwina mə=d-kowe ǧġaliyyat hawxa, hiye komer: ono kṭolabno šəbqono mas=səryoye.*

58. *koməṛ, koməṛ: kṭolabno šəbqono mas=səryoye d-aḥna səmlan hawxa appe, səmme ab=babonaydan d-əbʿiwa d-qŭṭli as=səryoye d-əzzənne mi=dŭkṯaṯe. u oməṛ: as=səryoye, hiye komaṛ, as=səryoye ġălăbe ʿamo d-əmmina b-qalita-wa.*[156] *ġălăbe d-əmmina b-ṣənʿa-yo.*[157]

59. *hawxa kmaḥke ǧare.*[158] *hiye komaḻḻan kŭl=gave … kurd-ne. hano kərd-ne.*[159] *hani t-arke kŭrmanǧ-ne. w at=tərk-sti kəmmi: u=ʿamo səryoyo, d-əmmina ʿamo d-maḥətle, d-markawle mdinoyuṯo u ʿamo ʿatiqo u ʿamo d-kətle lišono ʿatiqo w d-kətle makṯab zabno ʿatiqo, ak-kərd-sti w at-tərk-sti. ma hano mede šṛolo-yo.*

60. *w hani d-kŭl=gave d-əmmina t-kənno ʿmayye d-əmmina koṭəlbi kŭl=gave, u reyəs-yo, d-laltaḥ-tər mine-yo, u naqqawat a=ḥreni-sti, ar=rabonaṯṯe kəmmi: ṭəl.., aḥna kṭəlbina šəbqono mas=səryoye ʿal d-huwi mam=măsălătani d-əqṭılilan.*

61. *xəd mə́ḻḻilŭx bu=šawṭo maqəmlan qoyəmto yaʿni harke, bə-Dyarbakər. e yaʿni hŭl li=dărăǧayo aḥna kətlan ŭʿdo hne aʿmayye. halbat kito d-əmmina kito šəkəlat-sti, bam=mo ʿaṣro, ʿəsri d-lanne, kḥayri b-ʿayno ḥreto. an=noše kŭlle lappe yaʿni lə=kwe t-howən ṭawwe ẓatan.*

---

153 Cf.Tur. *silah* “weapon”.
154 Cf. Kur. *çûçik* “small, little”.
155 Cf. Tur. *reis* “person in charge, leader, chief”.
156 Cf. Tur. *kalite* “quality”.
157 Cf. Tur. *sanat* “craftmanship, skill”.
158 Cf. Kur. *car* “sometimes, from time to time”.
159 Probably mispronunciation *kurd-yo* is expected here.

62. *e, hawxa. kə́twaylan aḥna noqušo. lo meqəm tlat̠t̠=əšne hawi məqq.., ʿal, bə-Swičra hawi-wa hno, bə-Swičra hawi-wa ʿl-a=.., ʿl-a=.., ʿl-am=mĭnărat*[160] *dağ=ğwemə*ʿ*,*[161] *lo=maqblənne, rafarandəm*[162] *səmwalle lo=maqblənne bə-Swičra.*

63. *yaʿni mšayəlle mu=ʿamo lo=maqblənne. ánnaqa e, bay=yawmanək-wa at̠iwa tre, at̠iwa tlot̠o, tlot̠o dirak*[163] *lu=bayto, aḥna lawġal yat.., e ánnaqla aḥna yatiwayna lawġal bə-šṛolo šotiwayna qaḥwa. ḥəḷḷi at̠i tlot̠o mḥalle lu=tarʿo.*

64. *man-yo u=qašo t-arke? omaṇṇo: ono-no. maṛ mək=kəbʿat, mək=kəbʿutu? oməṛ, oməṛ: kutxu noqušo harke? omaṇṇo: e. oməṛ: hawo gdoratle! ʿayn hawxa! ono, ono hawino šăš*[164] *hawxa mine yaʿni. omaṇṇo: hano qay koməṛ hawxa?*

65. *omaṇṇo: qay? oməṛ: gdoratle! e omaṇṇo: qay? ʿal mən? oməṛ: bə-Swičra qay lo=maqballe a=.., ağ=ğwe.., am=manurat dağ=ğweməʿayd̠an, qay lo=maqblənne? aḥna-sti lə=gmaqəblina. gdoratle!*

66. *omaṇṇo: ma qay aḥna me Swičra at̠ina? omaṇṇo: aḥna ʿatiqe=d-arke-na yaʿni; ʿamo ʿatiqo; dŭkt̠o ʿatəqto: ʿito ʿatəqto. ma kibi dorene? yaʿni laybi dorena. g.., g.., i=dawla lə=kmaqəblo! oməṛ, oməṛ: gdoratla! yawme=d-əʿrəfto-wa u=yawmo d-at̠ən.*

67. *oməṛ: elŭx muhla*[165] *hŭl yawme=d-əʿrəfto! hat d-lo doratla gḥozat oməṛ. yaʿni hawxa mə́ṛḷeli, mhadadleli! bət̠ər ono qreli lu=polis. u=polis-te azzeyo mḥay.., mḥayṣele at=tlot̠o. bət̠ər, hiya halbat, ono, ono qrewoli, u=polis mḥayṣele at=tlot̠o, ono, ono meqəm d-əmḥayṣalle am=moratt̠e məṛ.., mšadarralli xabro.*

68. *əmmi: glozam dəʿrat xayifo bi=dăʿwayd̠ŭx, d-lo hat, disa mhadadalli, hat gḥozat yaʿni! dʿaṛ eba xayifo! əmmi, əmmi: d-mičoki bu=ḥăpəs hat kŭd̠ʿat! hawxa yaʿni disa tah.., hedodo.*

69. *edi ono, edi dəm.., i=naqla d-azzí li=maḥkăma, azzí li=maḥkăma mšayele mini oməṛ: hani mhadallalŭx? yaʿni obəʿ d-noḥəl ax=xabre yaʿni d-be mə-mə́ṛṛali, xabre=d-qaṭlo mede nafəq me femayye lo. hiye d-omaṛṛe. omaṇṇo: lo, bass mə́ṛṛali: gdoratla. qay bə-Swičra lə=maqballe? bi=maḥkăma.*

70. *qay lo=maqballe i=.., a=.., am=manurat dağ=ğweməʿ hat-ste gdorat hat̠e. gdoratla! d-əbʿat zŭx, zŭx maški d-əbʿat l-Awroppa, d-əbʿat l-Turkya, d-*

160 Cf. Tur. *minare* "minaret".
161 Cf. Tur. *cami* "mosque".
162 Cf. Tur. *referendum* "referendum".
163 Cf. Tur. *direkt* "directly".
164 Cf. Kur. *şaş* "confused, puzzled". Cf. also Tur. *şeş (beş görmek)* "to be completely mistaken".
165 Cf. Tur. *mühlet* "fixed period of time".

əbʿat lə=gḏaʿno l-ayko. gdoratla! yaʿni hŭl yawme=.., hŭl yawme=d-əʿrəfto huwwali muhla. me yawme=d-əʿrəfto hŭl yawme=d-əʿrəfto.

71. *e, məḷḷi lu=ḥakəm, omaṇṇo, omaṇṇo: aḥna, omaṇṇo: lo, yaʿni lanne, yaʿni lo=kəmdaʿeno aʿlayye ʿal mede. omər: qay? omaṇṇo: hani, yaʿni hawxa lə=kšəbhi noše hawxa ksaymi mede hawxa. qay noše, noše azzé li=ğāmye mḥarkənne ʿal hawxa mede.*

72. *edi mšayele mənne. ḥa omər: ono-sti haw … ono šteli, w ḥa omər: ono lə=gḏaʿno ono mə́ṛṛali bi=ğāmye hawxa, w ḥa omər lə=gḏaʿno mən. edi lo=ḥkimənne. mə=d-nafiqina aṯən ṭləbbe šəbqono mini yaʿni xəd dəmmat, hanək, at-tloṯanək.*

73. *xəd səmli ṭawwuṯo aʿmayye, yaʿni xəd dəmmat fayiši mnakfe. ṭləbbe šəbqono mini. omaṇṇo: hatu aṯitu mhadadxuli ma mə=gd.., ma mə=kh.., mə=ḥaqq kətwulxu aʿli aṯitu mhadad..,? əmmi: šəbqono latwaylan ḥaqq aʿlŭx. hawxa yaʿni, măsăle, ṣbuṯo hawxa hawiwo aʿmi, e.*

74. *ádšato hawiwo ṣbuṯo ḥreto aʿmayna. d-əbʿat d-ommanŭx-yo. ʿal, ʿal u=zʿurayḏi kibe d-ḥṣar=əšne. d-əzewa lu=maktap.*[166] *fayəš mu=hno, yaʿni ṭṛalle bu=səd.., ṭṛalle bu=ṣənəf*[167] *xəd kəmmina. mu=.., mu=dino yaʿni d-lo=.., d-lo=samwa u=dino di=hno, di=ṭayuṯo, yaʿni bu=maktap, d-lo=doraswo*[168] *ʿal u=.., ʿal i=ṭayuṯo.*

75. *ṭṛalle bu=ṣənəf bass hiye u=kaširo dan=naʿime kŭlle. ánnaqla azzí ono, omər, omər: baba mḥalaf u=maktabano diḏi. latyo ṭawwo. omər: kə.., omər: mbali l-ḥa ṭaw-tər. omaṇṇo, ḥəḷḷi kobəʿ ġălăbe omaṇṇo: ṭṛ=owe.*

76. *qayəm mḥalafli. kəzzí kəmbalne lu=maktap ḥreno. kəmmi fayəš, kəmmi: fayəš bu=ṣənəf, yaʿni fayəš bu=sədro. bann=arbʿo-wa fayəš bann=arbʿo. lo=fayət laḥ=ḥamšo. e qay? kəmmi: lo=kəḏʿina. gəzzŭx mšaylat mu=maktap.*

77. *azzí mšayeli mu=maktabayḏe kəmmi: aḥna-sti lo=kəḏʿina, ṭamo ksaymile. boṯər azzí disa əmmi: lo=kowe. layban, layban d-maḥtínale bu=maktab d-l=uḏʿina baḥ=ḥamšo-yo lo. hedi əmmi: zŭx; mšaḏarralli lu=hno ʿeloyo di=dawla, d-.., d-kəmminale, di=milli yetəm*[169] *d-kəmminale, di=dawla.*

78. *azzino, əmmi: zŭx s-u=.., lu=qaymăqām.*[170] *azzí s-u=qaymăqām əmmi: zŭx s-u=maktabayḏe, s-u=maktabayḏe t-kətyo bi=mḥallatxu,*[171] *li=dawla uʿḏo*

166 Cf. Tur. *mektep* "school".
167 Cf. Tur. *sınıf* "class".
168 Cf. Ara. *darasa* "study".
169 Cf. Tur. *milli* "national" and *eğitim* "education".
170 Cf. Tur. *kaymakam* "official charged with governing a provincial district".
171 Cf. Tur. *mahalle* "neighborhood, quarter".

mbadele u=sistam.[172] *maqqa d-azzí la=tkoṯe ammi: u=maktabayḏe. mu=maktabayḏe glozəm misəm u=medano.*

79. *azzí lu=maktap, disa ammi: lo, latlan ʿalaqa. azzí disa l-dŭkṯo ḥreto, hano d-kəmmile u=milli yetəm, hano d-kommaṇṇo, yaʿni i=dŭkṯo rapṯo d-Dyarbakər, d-koḥayri ʿl-am=maktābe.*

80. *hedi azzino, azzino l-tamo ammo: zŭx maṛ lu=maktabayḏe d-kətwa ebe meqəm, maṛṛ elən, maṛṛ, maṛṛ: hăka d-lo=.., hăka d-lə=mʿadluto, ṣ̌rolo du=naʿimayḏi, d-lo=musqutule bu=ṣənəf, ono b.., ono b.., gdobenalxu lat=tălăfəzyōne w lam=maḥkămat.*

81. *hedi mə.., azzí məḷḷi hawxa, məḷḷi: hăka d-lo=saymutu hawxa ono gdobenalxu li=maḥkăma wə gdobenalxu lu=tălāfəzyōn. edi báṯərke hənnək zayiʿi xəd dəmmat. ono ḥaqqliwayno yaʿni, bam=mo mo. qay, lanna mağbūr*[173] *d-yəlfina u=dino daṭ=ṭaye. aḥna lo=d-yəlfina u=dino daṭ=ṭaye kŭzzan lu=maktap.*

82. *xəd dəmmat ono ḥaqqli hənnək mağbūr səmme, qayəm səmme, d-ḥa … mʿadalle w hedi hawi. hawxa, yaʿni hēš hŭl əʿdo gʿayšina hawxa medone yaʿni. yaʿni laybŭx d-əmmat bam=mo mo xəd, xəd Awroppa, baḥ=ḥaye. ʿazqo-yo d-howe ẓatan.*

83. *bam=mo mo laybŭx d-əmmat yaʿni ḥa raḥa-yo. bam=mo kibŭx d-əmmat tmoni, anğax,*[174] *anğax, yaʿni šawʿi, tmoni aḥna raḥa-na yaʿni. lanna haqqa ṭawwe xəd dəmmat. hēš hawxa medone hne, hawxa măsayəl hawxa kowe hēš, xəd máḷḷilŭx.*

84. *ṭaw-tər me meqəm ḥsar=əšne-yo, yaʿni əšmo ṭaw-tər. čike mʿadəl yaʿni. ánnaqa lo=kəḏʿina, gmiʿadəl lə=gmiʿadəl. ʿal i=.., ʿal i=hno kfoyəš, ʿal d-əmmina, ʿal i=dawla, ʿal u=rišo daw=wazire, ʿal aw=wazire, ʿal i=dawla, d-əmbadli aq=qanunat, am=medone. l-gorān*[175] *di=medaṯe. i=naqlayo, kibən kibən saymi ṭaw-tər. ḥozina, ʿal Aḷoho.*

85. *hiya haymən, ko.., hawxa xət məḷḷŭx, komaṇṇo t-oweno moṛo l-ṛuḥi. w ḥatta u=ḥa, naqlawat koṯelan ḏayfe-sti kəmminanne hwayo moṛo r-ruḥayxo. yaʿni kŭḏʿi, d-əmmina kito, kŭḏʿi an=noše. gmiḏoʿi, d-aṯən me larwal. t-arke kŭḏʿənne taqriban.*

86. *mawxa, yaʿni kweli fəkər ʿal awxa w u=ḥa t-koṯe-ste kəmminale. u=ḥa t-koṯe-ste kəmminale ṭr=owe moṛo r-ruḥayye. kowe, yaʿni lattat bam=mo mo*

---

172 Cf. Tur. *sistem* "system".
173 Cf. Tur. *mecbur* "forced to, obliged to".
174 Cf. Tur. *ancak* "barely, hardly, only".
175 Cf. Kur. *gor* "according to".

raḥa xəd məḷḷi, bam=mo təšˤi, bam=mo, hawxa. lə=kwe raḥa. kwele fəkər u=insān yaˁni, məqqa d-əmmat.

87. *yaˁni mšiḥoyo-hat čunku ono, yaˁni k.., yaˁni naqqawat kowe măsayəl d-əmmina harke. ba hăka aṯi ḥa mḥélelŭx me bəṯrŭx, hăka hawi mede, hăka … ḥa kṯele hawxa fəkrat d-əmmina meqəm, harke, bu=.., bi=dŭkṯaṯe bass.*

88. *hiya haṯe d-əmmina, i=tašˤiṯaṯe w təšˤiyawoṯe ġer xəttaṯe d-əmmina d-hawi aˁmi d-əmmina, hani təḥwiṯo, d-ḥaqqatan təḥwiṯo d-hawi sayfo-ne. ba qay ḥkəmno măsăla? qay ono, ono ḥkəmno bi=maḥkăma? balki harke domaxwayno ḥăpəs, balki, balki məqṭalwayno, balki howewa mo medone yaˁni. ḥa lə=kḏəˁ.*

89. *yaˁni hani təḥwiṯo ṭawto-yo d-əmmina. w xut-taṯe w ġer xut-taṯe-sti kito. hani ṭawwe-ne am=medonani i=naqqa d-məkṯowi.*

6. Translation text 2

1. To be honest, the, well, what happened to me was a great issue, frankly. Sometimes I myself wonder and ask myself how I got away with it.

2. When, when I was put on trial, I believe it was three hundred and eleven, under Article three hundred and eleven.[176] This means, here in Turkey, when someone divides the people, makes the people rise against the state.

3. This means that I have divided the Syriac people, made them rise against the state of Turkey. Becau.., becau.., for this matter I was put on trial three times. I was put on trial three times in the high court,[177] what we call high court, the greatest one here, in Diyarbakir, in Turkey.

4. And the three times, as it is, of course known for you, politicians came and as we say, people of high positions came, from Sweden, such as consular, your foreign minister came, the one that later was murdered.

5. She came three times; such people of high status came three times. They attended my hearings and I was saved. You know, also other people here were put on trial according to Article three hundred and eleven, Turks so to say, in Turkey, people that were, such as our own prime minister. He was put on trial for the same allegations.

6. It was because of a couple of words, that were not his own and that other people had written, he was sentenced to jail. He was put in jail and he had to pay money. But I was saved. But of course, this did not pass that effortlessly. For this I thank all our people, all our people that stood beside me and assisted me and that rallied the whole of Europe for this matter.

7. Some people organized demonstrations, others did, for example some organized activities for my cause. Because of this, because of this, because of this I was saved. I thank our people very much and ...

8. And of course, the problem was a great one, as I mentioned. It shows that, that when I was not sentenced and not sent to prison; the court

176 Father Akbulut says here 311 but in fact he means 312 which also is mentioned earlier in text 1.

177 Diyarbakir's Second State Security Court.

was arguing for jail; and as I mentioned, there are quite many that had been sent to prison here, put in jail, which means that the issue of the genocide of our people is accepted.

9. And frankly since, as long as I remember I know that it happened, that there was a genocide of our people. But sadly there are some of our people, among our people, that still do not accept this fact. They still think that it did not happen.

10. According to me, the one who does not accept the fact that it did really happen, he is a trai.., these may be seen as, how shall I explain it to you, if I say traitor it won't be nice, but actually something similar. But on the other hand, they maybe are worried, that something bad will happen. Or they are anxious. Or … but sometimes one may think that they are correct.

11. But one should not be afraid. This is the truth. This is our history, our past. We cannot deny it either. We as Christians, if we have been slaughtered because we were Christians, because of Christ, we cannot deny it. Nor should we ever deny it, do you understand?

12. And so, after that I was saved from that trouble, I thank God that I have been saved without, what it is called, without, without any harm or any thing, and without dread. It happened that I have escaped and I thank God.

13. After that happened, there used to happen various things to us. There were times, so to say, the people that were here, of course at that time, not now since almost twelve years have passed since then, at that time they used to look at me with mistrustfulness. They observed me a lot.

14. You maybe have seen, heard, that some young men that passed the alley, back and forth, used to kick our doors, and that, and that, and they called us names. And there were some who used to throw stones from above, from the wall of the church. They used to throw stones on us and used to break, for example the windows. They used to cause us lots of harm, damage through these kinds of acts, at that time of course. Now it is better.

15. Concerning this I also can mention, I can give an example, once, once there were children, young men, let us say fourteen, fifteen year-olds, and also older, they repeatedly threw stones.

16. So once I went out and said to one of them: why are you throwing stones on us in this way? What have we done to you? I said to his family but they did not at all bother. They did not even look me in the

eyes, so to say. They did not care, as if they wanted to say: it is correct behavior towards you. You deserve to be hit with stones.

17. Yes, and sometimes, also a child used to toss stones. Again, again I went and said to his, because we used to see them here, around us, we knew who they were, I have been here for a long time, so I went and sai.., told his father. His father said: go away! In such bad way, brutal, such as, he said: go away! As if he said: get the hell out of here! Or something similar. Thus, of course, I left him.

18. And also one day, one day there was also someone, an old, a young man, he was a fifteen, sixteen year-old. He shouted at med: *papaz papaz*, which means "vicar vicar". Thus he made fun of me, so to say.

19. I asked: whose son are you? Where do you live? He rushed away. His friends said to me: he lives just here, go there! I went there and said: thus your son says to me. Also they, as if you would say, as if you would say, did not appreciate me, as if they did not care at all, as if you would say: whatever he did against you, you deserve it.

20. So truthfully, in such way we were exposed to incidents. And also one day we had, so to say, guests, visitors and we were sitting in the courtyard. You have seen our courtyard. In summer we usually sit out there. It was early evening and they threw stones. We went out. We wanted to see who they were and why they were throwing stones.

21. We saw immediately that they were almost, almost ten, fifteen young men armed with sticks, knives and such things. We did not, we did not even dare to approach them. We did not start to talk to them to inform ourselves about the reason. We had also guests sitting there and they were bewildered. They were astonished and wondered: how such things may occur, our sitting visitors.

22. And this kind of incident, such, we got used to it, as if one would say, it became normality for us. Every now and then when I went out they would say something bad; they would, for example say, *papaz papaz, gawər gawər. gawər* means that you do not believe in God, yes, so.

23. They often used such utterances when one passed. And one, and they used to toss stones at me, and they also threw stones over the chur.., over the chur.., over the wall of the church towards us. As I mentioned, they used to damage our windows and other things. They caused the church and us together much destruction. And they also used to hit against the door.

24. And also there were many of the Muslims here, originally, their origin still from the genocide, so to say victims of the genocide, many of

them, of their grandfathers and of their elders, they converted to Islam to escape the slaughter.

25. So these ones, their grand, their grandchildren, their grandsons, their grandchildren, so to say, that are still in life now, many of them, some of them were happy for what happened. It went so far that some come to me and congratulated me, meaning well done. They said: well done. What can they do to you?

26. And these are Christians by origin. There are many of them here. You may ask, why don't they convert back to Christianity? They just cannot. They are mixed with each other. But there are lots of them. One can now say that maybe up to fifty per cent of, believe me, should you ask them, their origin is Christian. But they wanted to escape the slaughter during the genocide.

27. Many of them take me as an example. Let me give an example concerning this. I will tell you something in this matter also. Once came a man to me. He was about a sixty year-old. He came and said to me: you are my uncle.

28. I asked: how is that possible? He said: you are my uncle. But how? He answered: my mother is one of you. But how? He answered, he said: once they organized a caravan, at that time it was named caravan, which means a gathering of people, groups, do you get it? Do you understand?

29. They organized them in groups and took them away, slaughtered them and came back. So he said: also my mother, once they took a caravan; this Muslim man is telling me, my mother was in this caravan. She was one of you. She was in this caravan. She also was one of those who were taken to be slaughtered. They took them, he continued, and there was a woman amongst them that was pregnant, in her 8th month, maybe.

30. He went on: the two soldiers that were guarding them started to argue, quarrel with each other. One of them said: it is a boy and the other one said: it is a girl, a daughter and one said: a son. Thus they quarreled a lot and at the end one of them seized a dagger and opened her belly, the, the woman's belly, the woman's belly and took out the baby (foetus) and said: look here! Is it a boy or a girl?

31. So imagine, the Muslims here relate these kinds of horrifying stories. So this story was told to me by a Muslim and they also come to me and tell many other similar stories. There are also these kinds of people

here, people that like us a lot. They say: you are good people. You are better than us. They utter such words.

32. And thus, there are many of them that are, as I said, Christians by origin and, yes. And moreover, there was another one, when, when I was released, when this issue arose, and not only them, but also, what are they called, they disagree with each other, the leaders in Turkey, they do not agree with each other. The relations between them are not good.

33. So these who belong to us, once I was on my way out, for instance, one of them came through the door and kissed my forehead, just like that; he was an elderly man. He was approximately seventy years old. He came forth and kissed my forehead and said: I am proud of you.[178] He continued: you did the right thing, as if he was encouraging me.

34. He said: you did the right thing. He went on: what can they do to you? Let them come and ask me, I too will say that there had been a genocide, and we, and we, our forefath.., our ancestors, our forefathers were Christians. Even he, the Muslim man told me so, and many others. And every single time he sees me, I notice that he still shows good feelings towards me, good contact.

35. So there are people of this kind, on the one hand, and there are also people that are the opposite, on the other. So now, the majority, one can say ninety percent, percent, or one may say eighty percent, ninety have changed. They have changed both between each other and towards us, towards the Christians also.

36. Nowadays, also in the municipalities I have contacts with them. And I furthermore, there is, there is, what we call council of the forty witnesses, I too am a member in that council. This means that the municipality takes my ideas into consideration, still until now. We have now a new council at the municipality but hopefully they will go on, continue the same way.

37. Whatever happens they consult us, for instance, is it better to act this way or is it better to, we have even raised a stele here, for the suppressed people here, the municipality here, together. It is for the sake of the people that have been suppressed, that have gone through lots of difficulties here. But it is not mentioned openly that it is for the genocide.

---

178 Lit. you are worth the both eyes.

38. Thus they do not say it openly. They only say: it is for the people that have been suppressed. It is written on it in Syriac, in Turkish, in Armenian, in Kurdish and in the languages such, it is written on the stele. Thus, so many things have changed.

39. We, let us say I, have a very good relationship with them. But of course, they did not change one, one hundred percent. One may say that the people here have changed up to eighty percent. And, and we have good contact with them and so on. Bu we, we the people that are living here, our people, the Syriac people, they are still, they are still not aware of, some of them are not aware whether there has been a genocide or not.

40. And they do not have, they do not accept, yes, there are some that have these ideas also. We have to, I mean the Syriac people, all of us, have to have the same approach, that we were victims of the genocide. When we were slaughtered, they did not slaughter some of us and spare some of us. The aim was to kill everyone, every single one of our people.

41. That is why we all should be together, strong in this, in this approach, united together. And this matter, as you already have seen, through my dispute about the genocide, and that had created a great echo, that was heard, every single one of us should work hard the same way. I mean that this has occurred, that this has happened to us, that we have been ethnically cleansed. Because our place of origin is here.

42. Our people, that we had here, we had an old history here. We have ancient roots here. We have ancient culture here. We have an old language here, so old that there is no older language than it in this region. It is we who gave name to this region. This is fact, it's geographical, the whole geographical term is Mesopotamia, and also what's inside of it.

43. It is we who gave these names. And this is evident, when you say the name of the region in Syriac, in, in, it is in our mother tongue. That's why we, we have to think in this way, give each other strength in this matter, get united in this struggle and so on.

44. And for us this is something that is one hundred percent indisputable. There is no, there is no, not at all, that, that we were not victims of the genocide. And even once it occurred here, actually, whatever happens now, since they know me, for instance, the lawyers, such as people that are, what is called, whoever meets me knows me, they say, when something particular arises, they want me to talk with them on television or something similar. They know. I talk to them.

45. They know, when they know what I have said, I mean I have become a symbol of this, the genocide. Sometimes they say, I say: God, one cannot every now and then, I, I, what is it called, am afraid of our own people and not of the state. So imagine, I am afraid of our own people.

46. If not, I am capable of saying it again. I mean I can speak of it again, give exposure again. So that's why they know me. You may say that I have become like a symbol of the genocide. Everyone knows, it is known both for our people and for whoever, for the educated, so to speak, for the educated, for the lawyers, for the, for the, for the enlightened ones between the people, both Turks and our people.

47. So, do you have any questions? Honestly, no matter how much I tell you, you would maybe think: he is patting himself on the back, but this is a great deal, not only for me; you know, they told me: withdraw your statement! Take it back! I mean the people here, our people, take it back or they will kill you, they will throw you in prison.

48. I answered: I am not in any way better than those who have been slaughtered so, I am not better than a single one of them. And they have put many in, they have killed them in prisons and in, what is it called? I said: let me also be one of those. I was thinking in this way. And furthermore, it was true.

49. When someone withdraws a historical statement such as this, I mean it will forever remain my own responsibility and this I consider as something immoral for my own sake. It would have been something immoral for my own person. But now, what I have stated, as I mentioned earlier, it turned out much better for me, but above all for our people. Concerning me, I am just a simple person, but for the people, for the genocide it turned out to be something positive.

50. Imagine that it might come time and for some reason, someone would say: at a certain time, this or that person, that priest, priest Yusef stated that the genocide really occurred and behold, nothing happened to him. See, in this way the path for the truth opens little by little, as one may say.

51. And there are many other lawsuits, for instance as this one and from which I have been saved, here in Turkey, and which drew interest, many other lawsuits, lawsuits are still at court, also about peoples, and individuals. They may for example say: but behold, in this certain lawsuit he had been in a court hearing.

52. The lawyers can for example say: a certain individual was heard in the court, a certain priest, but was not put in jail. This can be as an

example, an example for many other issues; it sheds light on other issues, other cases.

53. So they said to me: take back your statement! But not matter how much they asked me I did not even consider withdrawing my statement. Believe me, while I stood in the court, I thought for myself, how much we, just in my village, Iwardo, for example there three months of fighting.

54. And there are still bones, the bones are still there, spread in those places. The bullets from the weapons are still in the church, in the church of St. Hushabo, our church. It is there until this day. And the mother of, and furthermore, I, when I was still little, the mother of my father had experienced the genocide. She is also shown on television sometimes. She was shown on television.

55. She was distributing bullets, I mean she was helping. She survived the genocide and she used to tell us. She used to tell us. And not only what she told, but we also read, we read in the books and we read about that time. But she used to tell us while we were little. We remember that from the time we still were very little.

56. But now she has, of course, passed away, six, seven years ago. She used to tell us about the barbarism then. And as I mentioned many here now, there are many issues here, we hear about it from the Muslims. They tell us, they themselves.

57. We gather from time to time at the municipality, at the municipality, the head of the municipality, so once, I told you that I too am a member in the council, we gather and when these kinds of issues are spoken of, he says: I ask the forgiveness of the Syriac people.

58. He says, he says: I ask the forgiveness of the Syriac people for what we have done to them, what our forefathers did, that they wanted to slaughter the Syriac people so they would vanish from this region. And he continued: the Syriac people, he is telling, the Syriac people were of high quality. They are, for example, very dexterous.

59. Thus he tells. He tells us every now and then .., they are Kurds. This one here is Kurd. These here are Kurmanj. And also the Turks say that the Syriac people are the people who laid the fundament of civilization. It is the oldest people with the oldest language and that have ancient history. Both the Kurds and the Turks say such. Thus it is true.

60. So every now and then, since I am with them, they ask every now and then, no matter if it is the chief or if it is his deputy, and sometimes

also others from the elderly, say sor.., we ask the Syriac people for forgiveness for what happened, that we have slaughtered them.

61. As I mentioned earlier, we have raised a stele here in Diyarbakir. So this means that our cooperation with them is that good now. But of course, there are different kinds of people also, about ten, twenty percent of them are not, they see us with different eyes. All people cannot, as a matter of fact, be good.

62. Yes, so. We used to have a steeple. Was it not three years ago that a referendum, about, in Switzerland, there was, what is it called, in Switzerland there was about, about, about the mosque's minarets, they did not accept them, they had a referendum and it was not accepted in Switzerland.

63. They asked the people and they did not accept them. So it was at that time when two men came, three men, three came directly home while we were sitting inside, so we were actually sitting inside having coffee. I heard that three men came and knocked on the door.

64. Who is the vicar here? I answered: it is me. State your purpose, what do you want? He said, he said: do you have steeple here? I answered: yes. He said: you will tear it down! Just like that! I, I was confused because of that. I wondered why he is saying this.

65. I asked: why? He said: you will tear it down! I answered: but why? What is the reason? He answered: because in Switzerland, why did not they accept our mosque's minarets, why did not they accept them? We do not accept it either. You will tear it down!

66. I answered: but do you think that we come from Switzerland? I continued: we belong to this region since ancient times; we are ancient people; this is an ancient region; and this is an ancient church. Do you think that I can just tear it down? I cannot tear it down. It will, it will, the state will not allow that! He said, he said: you will tear it down! It was a Friday, the day when they came to me.

67. He continued: you have until Friday to do so! And if you do not tear it down, you will see. Thus he said to me, he threatened me, so to say! After that I called upon the police. The Police left and caught, caught the three of them. Then, as a matter of fact, I, I had called upon, the police caught the three of them, but before the police had caught them, their families said, sent me a message.

68. They said: you should immediately withdraw your claim, otherwise; they threatened me once again, otherwise you will see! Take it back at once! They said, they said: if they are to be put in prison you will see

what will happen to you! So once again in such way they threa.., threatening.

69. So I, so, when I was in court, when in court, I was asked: did these people threaten you? They wanted to hear extract the exact words, what they said to me, in case words of killing or so came out of their mouths or not. He wanted to tell them so. But I said: no, they just told me to tear it down. Why was this not accepted in Switzerland? This was in court.

70. Because they did not accept the, the, the mosque's minarets, you too will tear down this one. You will tear it down! And if you would like go, go and complain, and also to Europe, if you would like, and if you would like to Turkey, and if you would like, I don't know where to. You will tear it down. So you have until Fri.., you have until Friday to do so. This means, from Friday to Friday.

71. So I said to the judge, I said, I said: we, I said: no, they are not, I mean do not charge them for anything. He asked: why? I answered: well, these, they do not look like people that would commit such actions. Obviously some people, some people have been to the mosque and stirred them up to do so.

72. So he asked them. One of them said: I would never, I was drunk, and the second said: I do not know, while in the mosque they told me to do so, and the third one said I do not know what. So they were sentenced. When we came out of the court, they came forward and asked my forgiveness, so to say, those, those three men.

73. Because I have done them a favor, they were ashamed, so to say. They asked my forgiveness. I said to them: you came and threatened me, what, what, what right did you have to come and threaten me? They answered: we are sorry; we did not have any right to do so to you. So, this was an example of an incident that affected me, yes.

74. This year we suffered from another problem. If you would like I will tell you about it. It is about, about my son. He is almost ten years old. He goes to school. But he was kept in, what is it called, they kept him in the same cla.., they kept him in the back, so to speak. This was because of, because of religion, that he did not, that he did not attend, the, the teaching in Islam at school, that he did not study about, about Islam.

75. They kept him back in the same class even though he is the cleverest boy amongst all the children in his class. So I went, he said, he said: father I would like you to change this school of mine. It is not good. He

continued and said: take me to a better one. I noticed that he wants this very much so I said: let it be so.

76. So I changed his school. I took him to the new school. They said: he will repeat, they said: he will repeat the same class. He will repeat the same class. He was in the fourth class and stayed in the fourth class. He did not go on to the fifth class. I asked: but why? The answered: we do not know. You should go and ask the old school.

77. I went and asked at his old school. They answered: we do not know either. They should arrange it there. So once again I went there and they told me: it is not possible. We cannot, we cannot take him in if we are not sure whether he is in the fifth class or not. After that they said: go; they sent me to, what is it called, the state's highest, the, the, what we call, national education, as we call it, which belongs to the state.

78. So I went there. They told me to go to the, to the governor. I went to the governor they told me to go to his school, to his school that is in our neighborhood. The state has now changed the system. No matter how many places I went to, they all told me: his school. This must be rectified from his school.

79. I went to the school, and once again they said: no, it is not our concern. So once again I went to another place, this place that is called national education, which is a great authority in Diyarbakir, and that supervises schools.

80. So I went, I went there and she told me: go back to his old school and tell them, say, say: if you do not, if you do not rectify, honestly my sons, if you do not raise him up a class, I will, I will report you to the television channels and to the courts.

81. So I sai.., I went there and told them so, I said: if you do not rectify this matter I will report you to the court and I will report you to the television. So after that they were scared, so to speak. I was one hundred percent right. Why, we are not obliged to attend studies in the Muslims' religion. We do not go to school to learn about the Muslims' religion.

82. I was right, so to speak and they were obliged to do it, so they did it, so that, they rectified it and then it was done. As you see, even today we experience such harassments. One cannot say that it is hundred percent like Europe here, never. As a matter of fact, it is does not look like if it is going to be so either.

83. One cannot say that we are one hundred percent safe. One may perhaps say that we are safe up to eighty percent, hardly, hardly,

maybe seventy, eighty percent, that we are safe. We are not that comfortable, so to speak. These kinds of harassments, these kinds of issues still arise, as I mentioned to you.

84. Nevertheless, it is better than ten years ago, a little better, so to speak. It got a little better. But we do not know whether it will get even better or not. It all depends on the, on the, so to speak, on the state, on the prime minister, on the ministers, on the state, if they will change the law and such matters. It is according to this. If it would be so, then they can, they can make it better. We will see. May our Lord help us.

85. Actually, as you mentioned, I use to remind myself to take precautions. And also the one that, sometimes we receive guests who we tell to be careful. As a matter of fact, they know, I mean there are, they know the guests. Those who come from abroad are known. The people here, practically recognize them.

86. So that is why I am worried about this and advise those who come and visit us. So we also advise those who visit us to take precautions. So it happens, I mean, you are not one hundred percent safe, as I mentioned, maybe ninety percent or so. One is never safe. The human being in us worries, so to speak, no matter what.

87. At the end you are a Christian! Because I, I mean, sometimes things take place here. For example, imagine if someone approaches from behind and assaults you, if something would occur, or if ... so one thinks this kind of thing in advance, here, in this, in this region only.

88. As a matter of speech, this problem and other similar problems, so to speak, which occurred to me, are nothing else but evidence, evidence that shows that the genocide did surely take place. Why would I otherwise be dragged to court? Why did I stand in court hearings? I could have been sentenced to prison, maybe, I could have been murdered, and maybe one hundred other things could have happened to me. One will never know.

89. So one may say that this is a good way to inform people about what happened, and also other issues like this. These issues are helpful once they are written.

Idioms

Idioms in a language are always hard to render with full nuance in translation to another language. Therefore, some idioms from the Turoyo of ʿIwardo are also chosen to be rendered literally below.

Idiom	Meaning	literally
at=tarte ʿayne hat	I am proud of you	you are worth the both eyes
aṯi l-qamuṯi	he welcomed me	he came before me
xile ḥăpəs	he was sentenced to prison	he ate jail
nšəqle bayne=ʿayni	he kissed me on my forehead	he kissed me between my eyes
bə-qḏoli kfoyašwa	it would have been my responsibility	it would have stayed in my neck
lo=maḥətli b-hawni	I did not bother	I did not put in my mind
koṭəʿni ġamo	they worry	they carry anxiety
mḥalle lu=ṭarʿo	they knocked on the door	they hit the door
hawino šaš	I was confused	I became confused
ʿal mən?	why?	On, or about what?
d-lo hat gḥozat!	otherwise you will see!	if not, you will see
maqəmme orifi li=raġlo	they rallied Europe	they made Europe stand on the foot
dʿar bi=dăʿwaḏŭx!	take back your claim!	go back in your claim!

fayiši mnakfe	they got embarrassed	they stayed embarrassed
mə=ḥaqq kətwulxu aʿli?	why did you do that?	what right did you have on me
kibe d-ḥṣar=əšne	he is ten years old	he is of ten year
baḥ=ḥaye	Never	in the life
komaṇṇo t-oweno moṛo r-ruḥi	I should take cautious measures	I think of taking care of myself
kweli fəkər ʿal awxa	I worry about this	I have thoughts about this
aṯi sayfo aʿlayna	we were victims of genocide	a sword came over us
taḥt i=ʿayno	under surveillance	under the eye

Glossary

The glossary below contains words and word forms that are attested in the texts above. Verbs that are attested in more than one form are presented in the glossary where they can better be overviewed. If a noun is not explained, it stands in masculine. Feminine nouns are marked with (f.). When attested, all forms of the noun are given, i.e. masculine, feminine and plural (pl.). The order in this glossary is as follows:

a, ʿ, b, č, d, ḏ, e, f, g, ġ, ğ, h, ḥ, i, k, ḷ, m, n, o, p, q, r, s, ṣ, š, t, ṭ, u, v, w, x, y, z, ẓ, ž.

Many terms used in contact with police and other authorities, such as *dawla* "state", *maḥkama* "court", *ifada* "statement", *ʿalaka* "connections, tie, relationship", *baladiyye* "municipality", *mağlis* "assembly, council, board", *ğami* "mosque", *muhla* "fixed period of time", *mağbūr* "forced to, obliged to", *tarih* "history" etc. are of Arabic origin but used regularly in Turkish. In the footnotes I refer to them as Turkish and not Arabic since for me it is obvious that they found their way to Turoyo through Turkish. In cases where it is really clear that the loan-word is from Arabic I refer to is as such.

a

ʾabadan	never
abro, pl. *abne*	son
afandi	mister, gentleman
aġlab	majority; *aġlab mənne* the majority of them → *ġălăbe*
aḥna ~ *əḥna*	we
alfo	thousand
Aḷoho	God
amniyye	security
amṭe – *amṭele*	bring; *aṯən mṭallali lu=bayto* they came and brought me home
anğax	barely, hardly, only
ánnaqa – *ánnaqla*	now, so now, this time
arbaʿ	four
arbaḥṣar	fourteen
arbʿi	forty

armənoye	Armenians; *ann=armənoye* the Armenians, *u=ʿamo armənoyo* the Armenian people
asiruṯo	contact, connection
aṣāṣ	fundament, originally
avŏqate	lawyers
Awroppa	Europe
awwəl	first, at first
áydarbo	how
ayko	where; *hatu m-ayko-hatu?* Where are you from?
azzé – azzeyo	he went, left; *azzé mahzamle* he left and escaped; *u=polis-te azzeyo* also the police left; *azzí li=maḥkăma mšayele mini* … I went to the court and he asked me …; *azzino l-tamo* I went there; *azzən məṛṛe lu=mŭdūr* they went and told the chief; *gəzzŭx mšaylat mu=maktap* you will go and ask the school. Imperative: *zŭx! zŭx marke!* Go away! *iyzŭx lo=ṭorat məğğoli kŭrmānğï!* Go and forbid them to talk Kurdish!

ʿ

ʿal, aʿl-, ʿl-	on, over, about, against. With personal suffix: 3.m.sg. *aʿle;* 3.f.sg. *aʿla;* 2.m.sg. *aʿlŭx;* 1.c.sg. *aʿli;* 3.c.pl. *aʿlayye;* 1.c.pl. *aʿlayna; u=ʿamo səryoyo aṯi sayfo aʿle* genocide came over the Syriac people; *košapəʿ aʿla* it has passed over her; *latwaylan ḥaqq aʿlŭx* we did not have any right against you; *mqašmarle aʿli* he made fun of me; *lo=kəmdaʿeno aʿlayye* I do not raise a claim against them; *hawi u=medono aʿlayna* this happened to us
ʿălaqa	connections, tie, relationship
ʿam, aʿm-	with, together with; *aʿmi* with me; *əʿdo gdoṯat aʿmayna!* You should come with us now! *səmli ṭawwuṯo aʿmayye* I behaved well towards them
ʿamo, pl. *ʿame*	people; *u=qṭəl ʿamo* the slaughter, the genocide
ʿammo	uncle (on the father's side)
ʿaskar	military, soldiers
ʿaskariyye	military service
ʿasṛiyye	evening
ʿasṛo	ten
ʿatiqo	old, ancient

ʿoyəš - ʿayəš	live; experience; *hiya ʿayišole* she lived; *gʿayšina hawxa medone* we experience such things; *harke koʿayšina* we live here
ʿayn	exactly, just, so; *ʿayn hawxa mə́ḻḻile* exactly so I said to him
ʿayni	the same, equal, identical
ʿayno, pl. *ʿayne*	eye
ʿazquṯo	difficulty
ʿeloyo, f. *ʿelayto,* pl. *ʿeloye*	high
ʿəğbo	strange, wonder, unheard-of thing
ʿəsri	twenty
ʿito	church
ʿlaymo, pl. *ʿlayme*	young man
ʿobəṛ - ʿabəṛ	enter, come in; *ʿabiri li=maḥkăma* they entered the court
ʿoğəz - ʿağəz	*ʿağəzwayno* I had become exhausted
ʿoməṛ - ʿaməṛ	build, construct; *maʿməṛalle* they build it (f.)
ʿoyaqle - ʿayəqle	he did not like it; *ono mə=d-məḻḻi hawxa ʿayəqle hiye* when I said so he did not like it; *ḥəḻḻi koʿoyaqle, omaṇṇo: hăka lə=gmətyaqnat tŭx aḥna kətlan ʿito* I noticed that he does not like it so I said: if you do not believe, come we have a church
(yawme=d-)ʿrəfto	Friday

b

b-	in, with, (preposition); 3.m.sg. *ebe;* 3.f.sg. *eba;* 2.m.sg. *ebŭx;* 1.c.sg. *ebi;* 1.c.pl. *eban*
babo	father; *ab=babonayḏan* our forefathers
bahro	light
baladiyye	municipality
balki	maybe
basimo, f. *basəmto,* pl. *basime*	good, nice; delicious
barṯo	daughter, girl
bass	but; only
bayn	between, among, amongst; *baynoṯayye w aʿmayye* between them and with them; *u=xayin d-baynoṯayna* the traitor amongst us; *baynoṯayye-wa* he was between them; *aṯi nšəqle bayne=ʿayni* he came forth and kissed me between my eyes (forehead)

bayto	home, house
bele	yes, sure, of course; *omər: lo? omaṇṇo: e bele, tŭx əḥzayy!* He said: no? I answered: yes, sure, come and have a look!
Beṯ Nahrin	Mesopotamia
bəṯər	then, later
bə́ṯərke	afterwards, thereafter
bəᶜǧənwanne	they used to suffocate them
bolo	mind; *aṯi l-boli* it came to my mind (I remembered)
brindar	wounded, injured
briṯo	world, earth
buġro, pl. *buġre*	bullets, gravel

č

čaḥṣar	nineteen
čike	little, some
čoyək – čəkle	put in, inside; *čaykolŭx bu=ḥăpəs* it (f.) puts you in jail
čučəkāt	small, little
čoyər – čəḷḷe	tear, slit, split; *čəṛṛe gawa* they slit here belly
čunku	because

d

dăᶜwa, pl. *dăᶜwat*	trial, lawsuit, allegation
darġo, pl. *darġe*	step, stair, grade, degree, rank
dastak	permission, support
dawla	state
dayroyo, pl. *dayroye*	monk
de	come on! (strengthening imperative)
deri	in: *deri yawmo* the following day
dexono	smoke
dərto	courtyard
diḏ-	genitive exponent; 3.m.sg. *diḏe* his; 1.c.sg. *diḏi* mine; 1.c.pl. *diḏan* our
dino	religion
dirak	directly
disa	again, once again
diyalōġ	dialog
doᶜəṛ – daᶜəṛ	return, draw back. Imperative: *dᶜaṛ! dᶜaṛ eba xayifo* draw it (f.) back quickly!

doməx – daməx sleep; *daməx ḥăpəs w hule zuze* he was put (slept) in prison and paid fine (money); *damixi ḥăpəs* they were put in prison; *balki harke domaxwayno ḥăpəs* I could have been sent to prison because of this; *lə=ṭralle d-domaxno tamo* they did not allow me to sleep there; *gdomaxno čike* I will sleep for a while

dore – drele tear down, make s.th. fall

dorəs – drəsle study

dŭkṯo, pl. *dkoṯe* place; *ag=garme t-kofayši kalə́n ba=dkoṯanək* the bones that still remain are to be seen in those places

ḏ

ḏayfo, pl. *ḏayfe* guest, visitor

e

e yes

el- → *l-*

emo mother, *i=yemo d-babi* my grandmother (on my father's side)

esore connections, tie, bond

ə

əšmo little, some

əšmo, pl. *əšmone* name

əštaḥṣar sixteen

əšti sixty

əysīr prisoner, hostage

f

femo, pl. *feme* mouth

fəkər idea, believe

flān so-and so, a certain person or thing; *bə-flān zabno* at this or that time; *flān kess* this or that person

fohəm – fahəm, fhəmle understand; *fahimat?* did you understand? *kofəhmat?* do you understand?

foləġ - fləġle divide; *folaġ u=ʿamo* divide the people; *xəd*

	folaġno u=ʿamo səryoyo maqəmne mqabəl di=dawla t-Turkya as if (would) divide the Syriac people, raise them against the state of Turkey
folitiqore	politicians
fotəḥ – ftəḥle	open, open up; about telephone: call, dial; *koməftəḥ u=tarʿo hedi hedi* the door opens slowly; *omaṇṇo kfotaḥno tălăfōn lu=bayto* I thought of calling home; *ftəḥle tălăfōn* he 86alian the number. Imperative: *ftaḥ! ftaḥ məǧġal b-tərki ʿam u=bayto!* Call and talk Turkish with the family!
fot̠o	face
foyəš - fayəš	remain, persist, left; *bət̠ər kfoyašwa mede lo ṭawwo eli* it would have remained something bad for me later on; *ag=garme t-kofayši kalə́n ba=dkot̠anək* the bones that still remain are there to be seen; *hēš hŭl l-əʿdo kfayši* they persist until now; *fayiši mnakfe* they remained embarrassed; *fayəš bu=sədro* he remained in the (same) calss
fṣiḥut̠o	happiness, cheerfulness
fšiqo	easy
ftiḥo	open, openly

g

gab	by, beside, near. With personal suffix: 2.m.sg. *gabŭx;* 1.c.sg. *gabi;* 3.c.pl. *gabayye;* 1.c.pl. *gaban; naqqa at̠i ḥa gabi* once a man came to me; *gəmšudanno u-tălăfəzyōn gabŭx* I will send you the television (reporter); *kalino gabayye hŭl ṣafro* I stayed by them (police) until the morning; *ftəḥle tălăfōn lu=bayto, l-arke gaban* he called home, here to us; Often used with *l-*: *at̠ən l-gabi* they came to me
garak	necessary, must
garmo, pl. *garme*	bone
gave	instant, moment, time; *kŭl=gave* every now and then
gawər	non-Muslim, infidel, unbeliever
gawo	stomach; *b-gawe=t-Turkya* inside Turkey
gazeta (f.), *gazetat*	newspaper

gazəğatiyye	journalists
goran	according; *l-gorān du=medano* according to this thing (f.)
gorəš - grəšle	pull
gərobāt	groups
gunaydoġo	southeast
güwanlək	security

ġ

ġălăbe	many, much, a lot; *mərwayli ġălăbe medone* I had said many things. Elative: *aġălab*
ġamo	worry, concern; *ġamo layt(o)* it does not matter

ğ

ğaʿda	street
ğām, pl. *ğamāt*	glass, window
ğāmye, pl. *ğweməʿ*	mosque
ğare	sometimes, from time to time
ğəddayye	their grandfather
ğore – ğari	happen, occur, arise; *be məğ=ğarile?* What could have happened to him?
ğule (pl.)	clothes
ğumhūr bašqāni	president

h

hăka	If
halbat	certainly, of course
halxo, pl. *halxe*	walk, march
hanək	those
hani	these
harke	here; *ap=polis aṯən l-arke* the police came here
hano	this
haqqa	so much, that much
hat	you
-hat as copula	you are
hatu	you, pl.
-hatu as copula	you, pl. are; *ṭaw minan-hatu* you are better than us; *hatu m-ayko-hatu?* Where are you from?

haṯe (f.)	this
hawno	mind
hawxa	so, in such way
hayko	where → *ayko*
hayman	believe me
haž	awareness, information
hedi	then, and then; *hedi hawi ʿasṛiyye* and the it became evening
hedi hedi	slowly, gently, gradually
hēš	still
hənnək	they
hīč	nothing, none whatsoever
hiya	she
hiye	he
howe – hawi	become, turn into, come to be, come up, occur. With the prefix *ko-*: 2.f.sg. *kuyo*; 1.m.sg. *koweno; i=ʿito t-koweno eba hawila tralfo=šne* the church that I am at is two thousand years old; *waxta t-kowela tralfo=šne* it (f.) is becoming almost two thousand years; *mə=d-kowe ṯṛ=owe* whatever will happen, let it happen (I do not care the less); *lo=kowe d-əmmat medone mani!* You should (must) not say things such as these. *hawi ʿasriyye* it became evening; *u=ḥa d-hawi ṭayo xaləṣ* the one that became Muslim was saved; *hawi sayfo aʿlayna* a genocide was committed against us; *mə=d-hawyo i=saʿa traḥṣar mkamele* when it became twelve o'clock, he finished; *haṯe măsăle hawyowa ġălăbe rapṯo* this issue had become very big; *hawen ṭaye żboyəd lo=qəṭlənne* they became Muslims so that they won't slaughter them; *hawino xət t-əmmat sambol* I became, as you would say, symbol; *ṣbuṯo hawxa hawiwo aʿmi* such matter had happened to me
hno – hne	this or that; a word of confusion. The word is used when the speaker cannot immediately find words to express him- or herself
hŭl	until, as far as; *hŭl ṣafro* until the morning; *mofəqalli hŭl li=ğaʿda* they took me out as far as to the street
Hürriyet	name of a daily newspaper in Turkey

ḥ

ḥa, f. *ḥḏo*	one
ḥakəm	judge
ḥamməš	five
ḥamšaḥṣar	fifteen
ḥamši	fifty
ḥatta	even; *ḥatt məḻḻi hawxa* I even said so
ḥaṯo, f. *ḥaṯto,* pl. *ḥaṯe*	new
ḥăpəs	jail, prison
ḥaqq	right, correct, true; *ḥa kibe d-oballe ḥaqq-sti* one may also give them right; *hat ḥaqq-hat* you are right; *ono ḥaqqliwayno* I was right; *koṭəlbina u=ḥaqqayḏan* we demand our right
ḥḏoḏe	each other
ḥarayto	end
ḥasyo, pl. *ḥasye*	bishop
ḥaṭro, pl. *ḥaṭroṯe*	baton, stick
ḥawro, pl. *ḥawrone*	friend
ḥaylo	strength, power
ḥbušyo, pl. *ḥbušye*	jail, prison
ḥḏaḥṣar	eleven
ḥeḏorayna	around us
ḥəṣrono	damage
ḥfiṭoṯo	activities, actions, deeds
ḥiṣo, pl. *ḥiṣe*	hard, tough, firm
ḥokəm – ḥkəmle	penalize, judge, sentence; *lə=ḥkəmlali* it (f.) did not penalize me; *noše harke-ste ḥkim* also here someone was sentenced
ḥolo	uncle (on the mothers side)
ḥošu – ḥšule	think, regard, conceive
ḥoyər – ḥəḻḻe	look, see, watch; 1.c.sg. *ḥəḻḻi;* 3.c.pl. *ḥəṟṟe;* 1.c.pl. *ḥəḻḻan; ḥəḻḻi aṯi tloṯo mḥalle lu=tarʿo* I looked up and there were three persons coming, and knocked on the door; *ḥəḻḻan kalə́n kəppe balki ʿaṣro* we looked up and noticed that there were about ten people; *lo=ḥəṟṟe* they did not look up; *kḥayri b-ʿayno ḥreto* they look (at us) in a different way; *koḥayri ʿl-am=maktabe* they watch the schools
ḥoze – ḥzele	see, watch; 3.f.sg. *ḥzela*; 2.m.sg. *ḥzelŭx;* 3.c.pl. *ḥzalle;* 2.c.pl. *ḥzalxu.* Imperative: *ḥzay! ḥzéwayla u=sayfo* she had seen (experienced)

	the genocide; *ḥoziwaynanne harke* we used to see them here
ḥreno, f. *ḥreto,* pl. *ḥrene*	another
ḥṣar	ten

i

ifada	statement
inṣān ḥaqlări	human rights

k

kaččəke	girl
kalé	here he is (presentative particle); 1.c.sg. *kalí;* 3.c.pl. *kalə́n;* 1.c.pl. *kalán*
kallawat	money
kaširo	diligent
kaṯowo, pl. *kaṯowe*	author, writer
kawmo	pile, heap
kefo, pl. *kefe*	stone, rock
kibe	he can, he is capable; 1.c.sg. *kibi;* 2.m.sg. *kibŭx;* 3.c.pl. *kibən/kəppe*
kīt, kito	there is; *kīt mede ḥreno d-əmmat?* Is there anything else you would like to say? *kito hawxa šəklat-sti baynoṯayna-sti* also between them there are different kinds; *kətwa balki ḥamšo=što alfo šaxṣat* there were maybe five, six thousand people
kmiʿağabno	I wonder, get astonished
kofər – kafər	deny, refute, reject
kole- kali	wait, await, stop, stay. Imperative: *kluy! u=müdūr kokolelŭx* the chief is waiting for you; *kalino tamo* I waited there; *90alian tamo hŭl ṣafro* we stayed until the morning; *kali, law aḏəʿ mə=d-omər* he stopped and did not know what to say
kowe	become, happen → *howe – hawi*
kṯowo pl. *kṯowe*	book
koṯu – kṯule	write; 3.m.sg. *kṯule;* 3.c.pl. *kṯuwwe*. Imerative: *kṯaw! kṯuwwayle* he had written; *i=naqlayo kṯuwalle* … at that time they had written …; *me d-məḷḷi kṯuwwe* whatever I said, they wrote it

kuhno, pl. *kuhne*	a man of religion
kŭl	every, all; 3.m.sg. *kule;* 3.f.sg. *kula;* 3.c. pl. *kŭlle;* 1.c.pl. *kulan; kŭl=d-əkḥozeli* every time he sees me; *kŭlle ṭaye-ne* they all are Muslims
kŭltūr	culture
kŭrmānği	Kurmanji, north Kurdish

l

l-	to, for; 2.m.sg. *elŭx;* 1.c.sg. *eli;* 1.c.pl. *elan*
laf	towards
lalyo	night; *b-lalyo* at night; *i=saʿa hawyo ḥḏo du=lalyo* it became one o'clock in the night
larwal	out, outside
lawġəl	inside
layt(o)	there is not
lebo	heart
lešono ~ *lišono,* pl. *lešone*	language, tongue
lo	no
lowəš - lwəšle	put clothes on, get dressed; *disa lwəšli ğuli* once again I put my clothes on; *yaʿni d-kolawši səfil, ğule səfil* I mean those who dress civil, civil clothes
lozəm – lazəm	to be important, necessary: *kulan glozəm d-howina* … we all should be …; *ḥa lə=glozəm zoyəʿ* one should not be afraid; *glozam dəʿrat xayifo bi=dăʿwayḏŭx* you should quickly withdraw your claim; *mə=t-kolozəm kosaymina* whatever is required we do it

m

maʿ əl-ʾasaf	unfortunately
maʿmala	behavior
maʿna	meaning; *maʿnata eli fləġli as=səryoye* it means I divided the Syriac people
maʿraqalli	they made (let) me escape
mağbūr	forced
mağlis	assembly, council
mağre – mağrele	dare; *lo=mağrelan d-əmqadmina* we did not dare to go forward
mahzəm – mahzamle	flee, escape; *mahzamalli* they made (let) me escape

maḥət – maḥətle	put, place, add to, set; 2.m.sg. *maḥtat;* 1.m.sg. *maḥənno;* 3.c.pl. *maḥətte;* 1.c.pl. *maḥtina; aḥna maḥətlan a*ʾ=ʾ*əšmonani* we have put these names; *ono lo=maḥətli b-hawni d-do*ʿ*aṇṇo* I did not consider to withdraw; ʿ*amo d-maḥətle, d-markawle mdinoyuṯo* a people that set out, established civilization; *layban d-maḥtínale b-u=maktab* we cannot put him in school; *kito mede ḥreno d-maḥtat a*ʿ*la?* Is there anything else you would like to add to it? *maḥtalle* "*u=xayin d-baynoṯayna*" they put (published) it "the traitor among us"; *hani kŭlle ğğilinanne, mirili maḥtile tamo* we have spoken of all these, I said them and put them there.
maḥkăma	court
maḥke – maḥkele	tell, relate, narrate; *hano u=ṭayo komaḥkeli* this Muslim tells me; *aṭ=ṭay t-arke komaḥkən* the Muslims of here narrate; *hiya maḥkelalan ġălăbe* she told us a lot; *kŭl=gave maḥkiyowa eli* she used to tell me frequently
maḥkūm	sentenced, condemned
maḥwe – maḥwele	show, point out, demonstrate, seems like; *haṯe maḥwela hno rabo …* this showed a great …; *hani kŭlle mṭanne maḥwallan lu=ḥakəm* they brought all these and we showed them to the judge; *maḥwalle ḥaylo rabo* they demonstrated a great strength; *komaḥwe m-iḏət latwaylan ġălăbe …* it seems that because we did not have much …; *hat komaḥwe lo=kəḏ*ʿ*at …* it seems that you do not know …; *maḥwewalle* they had shown
maktūb	letter
makṯab zabno	history; *hano u=makṯab zabnayḏan-yo* this is our history
maktap	school
malḥo	salt
malkuṯo	paradise, heaven
malḷa	mollah
mamṭe – mamṭele	bring; *hani kŭlle mṭanne* they brought all these; *azzen d-moṭənne qayse* the went to bring themselves firewood
man	who; *d-man-hat?* To whom do you belong? *man komoḥe?* Who is striking?

maqbəl – maqbele accept; 3.m.sg. *maqbele;* 3.f.sg. *maqbela;* 1.c.pl. *maqbeli;* 3.c.pl. *maqballe*

maqəm – maqəmle raise up, cause to stand up; *maqimili ʿal i=dawla t-Turkya* I made them stand up against the state of Turkey

maṛ Ḥušabo St. Ḥušabo (name of the church of ʿIwardo)

maraq concern, anxiety

maṛḥəm – maṛḥamle show mercy; *lo=maṛḥimiwa appe* they did not show mercy towards them

măsăle, pl. *măsayəl, măsălat* issue, matter

mašhūr famous, known

maške – maškele complain, protest

maškəṛ – maškaḷḷe thank, show gratitude; *ono gmaškaṇṇo* … I thank …

mawto death

mazʿəq – mazʿaqle scream, shout, yell

maẓḅaṭa protocol, statement

mʿadəl – mʿadele correct, make right

mʿadrono helpful, supportive

mʿanət – mʿanatle disagree

mbadəl – mbadele change

mdaʿe – mdaʿele claim, request, demand

mdagəl – mdagele lie, deny; *lo=kəmdaganno* I do not lie; *laybi mdaganno* I cannot lie; *əmdagal u=mede d-məḷḷūx* deny what you said. Imperative: *mdagal!*

mdinoyuṯo civilization

mede pl. *medone* thing, something

meqəm before, earlier; *meqəm tlaṯṯ=əšne* three years ago; *meqəm d-əmḥayṣalle am=moraṯṯe* … before they captured their relatives …

mə what. This is a short form of *mən; mən-yo?* what is it? → *mən*

məftakər – məftakaḷḷe think, reflect, consider

məğġəl – ğġil talk, speak, state, express; 3.f.sg. *məğġolo;* 1.m.sg. *məğġanno;* 3.c.pl. *məğġoli;* 1.c.pl. *məğġolina.* With the prefix *ko-*: 3.m.sg. *koməğġəl;* 1.m.sg. *koməğġanno;* 1.c.pl. *koməğġolina.* Imperative: *məğġal! gməğġoli aʿmi* they speak with me; *kəbʿi məğġanno ʿmayye bat=tălăfəzyōne* the want me to talk with them on television; *ğġənno ʿam u=bayto b-səryoyo* I spoke with the family in Syriac; *hat áydarbo*

	gməğġolat səryoyo bu=bayto? How can you speak Syriac at home? *məğġəl b-tərki ʿam u=bayto!* Talk Turkish with the family! *u=gunaydoġu kule koməğġəl b-kŭrmanği* the whole southeast speaks Kurdish; *hat b-mən koməğġolat?* In what (language) do you speak? *lə=ğġilat, lə=gməğġolat tərki?* Didn't you speak, don't you speak Turkish? *balki lo=məğġolo aʿmi-ze* maybe she won't even speak to me *yatiwina ğġilina* we sat down and spoke; *ğġile hawxa mağġələnne* they talked in this way and made them talk; *hani kŭlle ğġilinanne* we spoke of all these; *ʿal d-koməğġoliwayna səryoyo bu=bayto ḥa mənne mʿanatle hawxa aʿmi, qḥir* because we used to speak Syriac at home, one of them was angry at me, he got upset
mən	what; *mən-yo?* what is it? *w ḥa omər lə=gḏaʿno mən* and one of them said I don't know what; *hat b-mən koməğġolat?* In what (language) do you speak? *mən d-oṯe qəm femi gdomaṇṇo* whatever comes to my mind (mouth) I will say it
məfṣəḥ – fṣiḥ	to be happy; *məfṣoḥiwa bu=medano* they were happy about this
məqḥər – qḥir	get angry, annoyed, irritated; *hiye qḥir ġălăbe* he got very angry; *qḥəṇṇo mine* I was angry at him; *ono qḥə́rwayno* I had become angry
məqšəṭ – qšiṭ	go away; *məqšat!* Go away!
mətyaqən – mətyaqanle	believe, trust; *hăka lə=gmətyaqnat tŭx* … if you do not believe, come …; *lo=komətyaqnat la-Aḷoho* you do not believe in God
məxləṭ – xliṭ	get mixed (with each other)
mğadala	dispute, wrangle
mğahəd – mğahadle	exert oneself, make an effort;
mhadəd – mhadadle	threaten
mhaləx – mhalaxle	walk, march
mḥaləf – mḥalafle	change
mḥalle	neighborhood
mḥarəb – mḥarable	fight, battle, struggle
mḥarək – mḥarakle	move, shake
mḥase – mḥasele	here: die
mḥayḏe	united
mḥayṣəl – mḥayṣele	find, grip; hold

mĭnărat ~ manurāt (pl.)	minaret
misəm	to be done; → *soyəm – səmle*
mkaməl – mkamele	end, finish, conclude; *i=saʿa traḥṣar mkamele i=maẓbaṭa* at twelve o'clock he finished the protocol; *d-qəḍṛiwa gəmkamliwa kule* if they would have been able to, they would have finished them all; *tre yarḥe kamile mḥarabbe b-ʿIwardo* three whole months they fought in ʿIwardo
mnakfo, pl. *mnakfe*	ashamed, embarrassed
mo	hundred; *bam=mo* hundred percent
mobəl – mbele	take, take with, take with by force; *naqqa mballe qafle* once they took a caravan; *məbliwa an=noše qəṭliwanne* they used to take the people and slaughter them; *tro mublilŭx* let them take you home; *mballali li=maḥkăma* they took me to the court; *hiya-sti ḥḏo manək d-mitawbəlowa lu=qatlo-wa* she also was one of those who were taken to be slaughtered; *mbali l-ḥa ṭaw-tər* take me to a better one; *kəzzí kəmbalne lu=maktap* I go and take him to the school; *aṯutu mi=ʿito mbalxŭli* you came and took me from the church; *at=tranək d-məblənne səmme mqarrasiyye* those two who took them quarreled
mofəq – mofaqle	take out; *mofəqalli hŭl li=ğaʿda* they took me out, all the way to the street; *i=tfəngayḏe bu=zor məfqalle m-iḏe* with difficulties they released his rifle from his hands; *məfqənne* they took them out
moḥe – mḥele	beat, hit, strike, throw; *mḥélelŭx me bəṯrŭx* he hit you from behind; *qay gmoḥat kefe?* Why are you throwing stones? *koḥozina qay komoḥən* we see why they are throwing stones; *moḥənwa kefe eban* they used to hit us with stones; *mḥeli ʿal u=ṭarʿo du=mŭdūr* I knocked on the chief's door; *ḥa naʿimo mḥewo disa kefe* a child was once again throwing stones
moqəḏ – moqaḏle	burn; *moqaḏlŭxlan* you have burned us
moral	courage, support
mosəq – mosaqle	raise, take up
moṭe – maṭi	arrive, reach; *maṭina l-su=mŭdūr* we arrived at the chief

moyəd – mədle	take, grasp; *mədle m-iḏi* he took it from my hand. As inchoative: *u=ḥakəm mədle qrele i=gazetayo* the judge took and read that news paper
mqadəm – mqadamle	come forward, draw close
msaᶜdono	helpful, supportive
msawyo	directly
mṣale – mṣalele	pray; *b-səryoyo komṣalina* we pray in Syriac
mṣawər – mṣawarle	take photo; *mṣawər qull ᶜayni* I imagined (pictured before my eyes
mšaḏər – mšadaḷḷe	send
mšawər – mšawarle	consult; *kəmšawri eban* they consult us
mšayəl – mšayele	to ask; *mšayele* he asked; *troṯən mšayli mini* let them come and ask me; *gəzzŭx əmšaylat mu=maktap* you should go and ask the school
Mšiḥo	Christ
mšiḥoyo, pl. *mšiḥoye*	Christen
mŭdūr	chief, head, director
muhla	fixed period of time
mqašmaḷḷe	make fool of s.o.

n

naᶜimo pl. *naᶜime*	little, small
nahiro, pl. *nahire*	enlightened
naqqa ~ *naqla* (f.), pl. *naqqawat* ~ *naqqat*	once; *i=naqlayo* at that time
Ndaṯalo	Virgin Mary, lit. God bearer < Syr. **yoldāṯ Aḷoho*
naxwaš	bad, ill
nofəq – nafəq	come out, go out; 3.f.sg. *nafiqo;* 2.m.sg. *nafiqat;* 1.m.s *nafəqno;* 3.c.pl. *nafiqi;* 1.c.pl. *nafiqina; xabre=d-qaṭlo mede nafəq me femayye?* Did they express any words of killing? *mə=d-nafiqina aṯən ṭləbbe šəbqono mini* when we came out they approached me and asked my forgiveness; *bəṯər b-yawmo nafiqi* one day later they came out; *deri yawmo nafiqo bi=.., bi=gazeta* the following day it (f.) was published in the newspaper; *hēš lo=nafiqat larwal harke?* Have you not come out here yet? *lo=nafəqno* I have not gone out; *kŭl=gave d-əmmina gnəfaqtwa gdəmmiwalŭx xabro*

	everytime, so to speak, you would go out and they would say things (words) to you; *mofaqle u=naʿimo* he took the child out
noqušo	steeple
normal	normal
noše pl.	people
nošəq – nšəqle	kiss
nufūs	identification card
număra	number
nŭxroyo	strange, stranger, foreigner

o

obe – hule	give. With the prefix *ko-*: 2.c.sg. *kobat;* 1.c.pl. *konbina; kobina vergi* we pay taxes; *kobat hno, dastak?* Do you give your permission? *qana d-l=obən kallawat lu=taqsi* so that they do not pay money to the taxi. With the future prefix *gd-*: *me qime gdobat i=yfada!* You will give your statement while standing; *gdobenalxo lat=tălăfəzyōne* I will give you (send you) to the television (reporters); *ḥa kibe d-oballe ḥaqq* one may give them right; *kibi d-obeno ṭofṣo* I can give an example
obəʿ - abəʿ	want; *obəʿ d-noḥəl ax=xabre* he wanted to extract the words; *áydarbo d-əbʿat* however you want; *əbʿi d-qŭṭli kŭlle* they wanted to slaughter all of them; *kobəʿ ġălăbe* he wants a lot; *mək=kəbʿuto?* What do you (pl.) want? *kəbʿina d-əmmina* … we would like to say …; *kəbʿi d-gurši ṣərṭo elŭx* they want to take a photo of you
oḏəʿ - aḏəʿ	know. With the prefix *ko-:* 2.c.sg. *kəḏʿat ~ kŭḏʿat;* 1.m.sg. *koḏaʿno;* 3.c.pl. *kŭḏʿi;* 2.c.pl. *kŭḏʿuto; lo=kəḏʿat* you do not know; *lo=kəḏʿoli* she does not know me; *an=noše kŭlle kŭḏʿi* everyone knows; *noše lə=gḏəʿ ma=qṭilile* no one knows who killed them; *d-mičoki bu=ḥăpəs hat kŭḏʿat!* If they would go to jail, you will know (see what will happen)! *kŭḏʿinanne* we know them; *law aḏəʿ mə=d-omər* he did not know what to say
omər – məḷḷe (məṛle)	say, tell, narrate; 1.c.sg. *məḷḷi;* 3.c.pl. *məṛṛe.*

	With the prefix *ko-:* 3.m.sg. *komər̥;* 2.c.sg. *kəmmat;* 3.c.pl. *kəmmi;* 1.m.sg. *komaṉṉo*. With the future prefix *gd-*: *gdomaṉṉo* I (m.) will say; *gdəmmi* they will say. Imperative: *mar̥*! With suffix: *maḻḻi*! Say to me! *kəmminale* we call it; *kəmmile* they call it. *xəd dəmmat* as if you would say. *mək=kəmmat ʿal u=qṭul ʿamo?* What do you say about the slaughter of the people? Negation: *lo=kəmmi* they do not say. *əmmiwa* they used to say; *əmmiwayla* they used to call it; *əmmiwaylan* they used to say to us; *gdəmmiwalŭx* they would have said to you; *mə́r̥r̥alŭx* they said to you; *ono mərwayli aqqa medonani* I had said all these things.
Omiḏ	The historical name of Diyarbakir
ono	I; *ono-no* I am; *ono-ste* I too
orḥe	guests, visitors
orifi	Europe
oṯe – aṯi	come; 3.f.sg. *aṯyo;* 1.m.sg. *aṯino;* 3.c.pl. *aṯən;* 2.c.pl. *aṯutu;* 1.c.pl. *aṯina.* With the prefix *ko-*: 3.m.sg. *koṯe;* 3.c.pl. *koṯən;* With the future prefix *gd-*: 2.c.sg. *gdoṯat* you will come. Imperative: *tŭx*! *naqlawat koṯelan ḏayfe* sometimes visitors come to us; *u=ḥa t-koṯe-ste kəmminale* we also say to whoever comes to us; *tro=ṯən mšayli mini!* Let them come and ask me! *aṯiwa ʿamo ġălăbe* lots of people had come; *i=wazərto barayto aṯyowa* the foreigner minister had come; *oṯənwa məbliwa hēš* they used to come and bring more; *ṣafro d-oṯeno b-imomo lə=kowe?* Is it not possible that I come tomorrow during the day? *xayifo glozəm d-oṯat* you should come quickly; *mən d-oṯe qəm femi gdomaṉṉo* I will say whatever comes to my mind (lit. my mouth)
oxəl – xile	eat. In the expression *xile ḥăpəs* means: he was sentenced to prison

p

păpāz	priest, minister, pastor
parlamanto	parliament
pire	here: woman, wife

polis	police

q

qadro	value
qáfla pl. *qáflat*	caravan
qaḥăr	anger, fury; *b-qaḥăr* furiously
qaḥwa	coffee
qalita	quality
qamayto	first, at first, at the beginning; *hŭl li=maḥkăma qamayto …* until the first hearing …; *hawi ṭawwo eli, lu=ʿamayd̲an qamayto* it became good to me but above all to our people; *aq=qamoyayd̲an mšiḥoye-wayne* our first ones (ancestors) were Christians
qamḥo	flour
qamut̲o	before, in front of; *at̲i l-qamut̲i* he came before me (welcomed me)
qana	for, for the sake of (introduces final clauses)
qaroyo, pl. *qaroye*	educated
qašo	vicar, priest
qašišo	vicar, priest
qašto	grandmother; *i=qaštat̲t̲e* their grandmother
qaṭlo	killing; *qṭəl ʿamo* genocide
qay	why
qaymăqām	official charged with governing a provincial district
qayse	wood, firewood
qayṭo	summer
qd̲olo	neck, throat
qimo, pl. *qime*	standing
qodəṛ – qadəṛ	to be able to, capable, *lo=quḍrina* we cannot
qonṣoloṣ	consul
qore – qrele	read; call upon s.o. 1.c.sg. *qreli;* 1.c.pl. *qrelan.* With the prefix *ko-*: 3.m.sg. *koqore; u=ḥakəm mədle qrele i=gazetayo* the judge took and read that newspaper; *qrelan ba=kt̲owe* we have read in the books; *u=polis koqorelŭx* the police is calling upon you; *i=yfadayo kula koqorela* he is reading all that statement; *qqoreno hat məḻḻŭx am=medonani kŭlle* I am reading that you have said all these things
qoṭəl – qṭile	kill, slaughter; *u=ḥa d-qoṭəl šawʿo mšiḥoye gəzzé*

	li=malkuṯo the one who kills seven Christians he will go to paradise; *noše lə=gḏəʿ ma=qṭilile* no one knows who killed them; *aḥna i=naqqa d-əqṭilina lo hən minan qṭil w ṭralle hən* when we were slaughtered, they did not slaughter some of us and saved others; *i=naqqa d-əqṭiḷənne lo=məṛṛe: hani bass qquṭḷina* when they slaughtered them, they did not say: we will slaughter only these; *qŭṭliwanne* they used to kill them; *balki məqṭalwayno* I could have been killed; *hayo d-əqṭilalle* that whom they killed
qoyəm – qayəm	stand, stand up. Imperative: *qəm! qəm! hawat mašhūr* stand up! You have become famous. As particle: then, so: *qayəm disa lwəšli ğuli* then, once again I put my clothes on; *qayəm yatiwina side* so we sat by him, (in his office)
qoyəmto	stele
qriṯo	village
qum- ~ qəm-	before, in front of, near, close; *qumi* before me *qəm ʿaṣriyye. nafiqina* before (close to) the evening we went out

r

rabo, f. *rapṯo,* pl. *rabe*	big, large, old; *u=rabo d-Dyarbakər* the greatest in Diyarbakir
rafarandəm	referendum
raġlo	foot; leg
raḥa	comfortable, fine, good; *kalí raḥa-no* see, I am fine
raportaže	reports
rapso, pl. *rapsat*	kick
rayis	person in charge, leader, chief
rišo	head, president, leader; *u=riš waziro diḏan* our prime minister;
ṛoḥəm – ṛḥəmle	like, love; *lo=rḥəmle qay yaʿni komaṇṇo: i=dŭkṯayḏan harke-yo* he did not like it when I said: our place is here
ruḥo	self, spirit, soul: *mu=yawmo d-koḏaʿno ruḥi* from the very first day that I knew myself; *hwayo moṛo r-ruḥayxo* take care of yourselves; *kəmminale ṭr=owe moṛo r-ruḥayye* we advise them to take care of themselves

s

saʿa pl. *saʿayat*	hour, clock
săbab	reason
sambol	symbol
sayfo	sword, refers to the genocide
sədro	class
səfil	civil; *səfil polis* civil police
sfar yawme	newspaper
side	at him, at his place, by him; *yatiwina side* we sat at his place
silāḥ	weapon
sistam	system
skino, pl. *skine*	knife
sniġro, pl. *sniġre*	lawyer
soyəm – səmle	do, make; 2.m.sg. *səmlŭx;* 1.c.sg. *səmli*; 3.c.pl. *səmme;* 1.c.pl. *səmlan;* With the prefix *ko-*: 2.c.pl. *kosaymat;* 1.c.pl. *kosaymina.* Negated imperative: *lo=saymat!* Do not do! *saymiwa* they used to do; *səmwalle* they had done; *mə-ksaymi?* What are they doing? *məs=səmlan ebŭx?* What have we done to you? *xəd səmli ṭawwuṯo aʿmayye* as if I have done something good with them; *saymiwanne qáflat quṭliwanne* they used to gather them in caravans to slaughter them; *áydarbo gsaymət mede hawxa?* How can you do something like this? *aḥna kosaymina ʿaskariyye* we do military service.
sūğ	guilt, fault, blame
suryoyo ~ *səryoyo*	Syriac; *u=ʿamo suryoyo* the Syriac people; *ğġənno ʿam u=bayto b-səryoyo* I spoke with the family in Syriac
Swičra	Switzerland

ṣ

ṣafro	morning; tomorrow; *hŭl ṣafro* until the morning; *ma ṣafro d-oṯeno b-imomo lə=kowe?* Would it not be all right if I would come tomorrow during the day?
ṣawʿoṯe	his fingers
ṣawği	prosecutor

ṣbuṯo, pl. *ṣəbwoṯo* issue, matter
ṣənʿa craftsmanship, skill
ṣənəf class
ṣərṭo photo, picture
ṣlibo crucifix, cross
ṣoxəṛ – ṣxəṛle close, shut; *ḥa mənne ṣxəṛle u=tălăfōn* one of them hang up the telephone; *qquṭḷilŭx kṣuxṛi i=ʿito* they will kill you and close the church; *ṭro ṣuxṛi i=ʿito* let them close the church; *hăka ʿal foṯi d-məṣxoṛo i=ʿito ṭro=qəṭ.., ṣuxṛila* if it is because of me the church will be closed, let them kil.., close it
ṣoyəm – ṣayəm fast, fasting; *kito hən d-ṣayimiwa* there were some who had fasted
ṣuroyo Christian

š

šaʿuṯo, pl. *šaʿuṯe* yellow
šāš confused, puzzled
šato (f.), pl. *əšne* year; *ádšato* this year
šawʿi seventy
šawʿo seven
šawṭo while, some time; *xəd məḷḷi bu=šawṭo* as I said a while ago
šaxṣ, pl. *šaxṣat* person
šēṯ six
šəbhoro honor, pride
šəbqono forgiveness, sorry
šəkəl way, manner, method; *məš=šəkəl gəzzŭx?* How, in which way are you going to leave? *komaṇṇo məš=šəkəl xaləṣno mina* I wonder how I could escape it; *məš=šəkəl d-omaṇṇŭx?* In which way can I explain to you? *məš=šəkəl kowe?* How can this be?
šəršo root, origin
šlomo, pl. *šlome* greetings; peace
šobəh – šabəh be like, resemble
šoməʿ - šaməʿ hear; 1.m.s *šaməʿno;* With the prefix *ko*-: 3.c.pl. *kšəmʿi;* 1.c.pl. *kšəmʿina; gšəmʿo briṯo kula* the whole world will hear; *gmašmaʿno qoli b-əbriṯo kula* I will let my voice to be heard all over the world; *xəd əḥzelŭx bi=ṣbuṯayo diḏi, du=sayfo d-*

	əšmiᶜo ġălăbe, šmiᶜowa as you have seen in my issue that was heard a lot, it was heard; *ono šaməᶜwayno ġălăbe medone* I had heard many things
šoməṭ – šməṭle	pull off, slit out
šote – štele	drink
šṛolo	true, right, correct, truly, accurate, *mede šṛolo-wa* it was something true, *šṛolo gawro ṭawwo-hat, iyzŭx* … if you are truly a good man, go …
šuṛo	wall
šuwole	questions
šwaᶜ	seven

t

tahlŭkat	danger
taḥt-	under; *taḥt i=ᶜayno* under surveillance (lit. under the eye)
tălăfəzyōn	television
tălăfōn	telephone
tām	whole, full, complete, perfect
tamo	there
taqriban	approximately
taqsi	taxi
tarᶜo	door
tarix	history
tašᶜiṯo, pl. *təšᶜiyawoṯe*	story, issue, matter
tavda	together
tawdi	thanks
təšᶜi	ninety
tfənge	rifle, gun
tlaṯmo	three hundred
tloṯo	three
tmanyo	eight
tmoni	eighty
traḥṣar	twelve
tralfo	two thousand
tre	two
tŭx	come! Imperative of *oṯe – aṯi;* pl. *toxu*

ṭ

ṭarᶜo	door, gate

ṭaw (m-)	better (than)
ṭawwo, f. *ṭawto,* pl. *ṭawwe*	good, well, fine
ṭayo pl. *ṭaye*	Muslim
ṭayuṯo	Islam
ṭʿənto	pregnant
ṭoʿən – ṭʿənle	carry; *koṭəʿni ġamo* the worry (lit. carry anxiety)
ṭofso	example
ṭoləb – ṭləble	demand, request, ask; *koṭəlbina u=ḥaqqayḏan* we demand our right
ṭore – ṭrele	keep, save, spare, leave; *lo hən minan qṭil w ṭralle hən* not only some of us were slaughtered while they saved the others; *ṭralle bu=ṣənəf* they kept him in the (same) class; *ṭro fotəḥ!* Let him open!
ṭowər – ṭwəḷḷe	break, smash, crash
ṭr=owe	let it be so, < *ṭro howe*

u

ŭʿdo - əʿdo	now

v

vergi	taxes

w

waxt	time; *mu=waxt du=sayfo* from the time of the genocide
waziro, f. *wazərto,* pl. *wazire*	minister
wuždān	conscience

x

xabro, pl. *xabre*	word
xanǧar	dagger
xayifo	swiftly, quickly
xayin	traitor
xoləṣ – xaləṣ	save, avoid, escape; *xaləṣno* I was saved
xŭd, xəd,	like, as, such as; *hawi ʿasriyye xŭd ŭʿdo* it became evening like now; *xŭd kŭḏʿutu* as you

	know; *xəd məḷḷi* as I said; *aḥna xəd əmšiḥoye* we as Christians

y

ya … ya	either or
yaʿni	which means, so to say
yarḥo, pl. *yarḥe*	month
yarixo, pl. *yarixe*	long
yawmo	day
yawo	see here, look here
yoləf – yaləf	learn; *yalifiwayna* we had learned
yotu – yatu	sit, sit down, take a seat; *azzino yatuno* I went and sat down; *yatiwina žġilina* we sat down and talked; *bi=dərto yatiwayna* we were sitting in the inner yard; *kə́twaylan ḏayfe-sti yatiwe* we also had guests who were seated; *aḥna yatiwayna lawġal* we were seated inside. Imperative: *ytaw! zŭx ytaw tamo!* Go and sit there!
yoru – yaru	become big, huge; *i=măsăle yariwo* the issue became huge

z

zabno	time
zangin	wealthy, rich
zʿuro	small, little; *u=zʿuraḏi* my child
zəd, zət	more; *ma zət, mede zət-tər mu=mawto layto* well, more than, there is nothing more than death
zədqe nušoye	human rights
zəḥṯo	fear, dread, anxiety
zlām	man
zobəṭ – zbəṭle	catch, grip, hold, grasp; *zbəṭle b-maẓḅaṭa b-ḥaqq diḏi* he held a protocol (registered a claim) against me; *zbəṭla d-əmmina bahro l-dăʿwat hēš* it (f.) grasped light (gave hope), so to speak to other issues
zor	difficult; *bu=zor* with difficulties
zoyəʿ - zayəʿ	be afraid, horrified;
zuze	money

ẓ

ẓatan	in any case, as a matter of fact
ẓlimi	be oppressed; *aʿ=ʿame d-əẓlimi* the people that have been oppressed

ž

žboyəd	for, for the sake of

References

Aktar, A. 2009. "Turkification" Policies in the Early Republican Era. In *Turkish Literature and Culture Memory: »Multiculturalism« as a Literary Theme after 1980.* Edited by Dufft, C. Wiesbaden.

Armale, I. 1919 (reprinted 1970). *Al-Qusara fi nakabat al-nasara* [The catastrophe of the Christians]. Beirut.

Armale, I. 2005. *De kristnas hemska katastrofer: Osmanernas och ung-turkarnas folkmord in norra Mesopotamien 1895 / 1914-1918.* Södertälje.

Arnold, W. 1989. *Lehrbuch des Neuwestaramäischen.* (Semitica Viva 1). Wiesbaden.

Arnold, W. 2000. The Arabic dialects in the Turkish province of Hatay and the Aramaic dialects in the Syrian mountains of Qalamûn: two minority languages compared. In *Arabic as a Minority Language,* edited by Jonathan O., Berlin – New York.

Ballı, R. 1991. *Dosyası Kürt.* Istanbul.

Bar-Dawud, Š. och X. 2013. *Ciwardo: Me at̠mël l adyawma, mën hawi? Damografi, Dabara, Sayfo w Golut̠o.* Södertälje.

Bengtsson, B. 2004. *Svärdets år. Om folkmordet på de kristna i Turkiet 1894 – 1922.* Södertälje.

Bezold, V. 2012. *Überarbeitung und digitalisierung des Ṭuroyo-Wörterbuchs von Hellmut Ritter.* Master's dissertation. Philosophische Fakultät II, Friedrich-Alexander University. Nürberg - Erlangen.

Bet̠-Şawoce, J. 1012. *Xëzne d xabre Ordlista: Şurayt-Swedi (mëd̠yoyo).* Stockholm: Författarens Bokmaskin.

Chyet, M. L. 2003. *Kurdish - English Dictionary.* London.

Costaz, L. 1986. *Syriac - English Dictionary.* Beyrouth.

De Courtois, S. 2004. *The forgotten Genocide: Estern Christians, The Last Arameans.* New Jersey.

Donef, R. 2009. *Massacres and Deportation of Assyrians in Northern Mesopotamia, Ethnic Cleansing by Turkey.* Södertälje.

Gaunt, D. 2006. *Massacres, Resistance, Protectors: Muslim-Christian Relations in Eastern Anatolia During World War I.* New Jersey.

Gaunt, D. 2015. The Complexity of the Assyrian Genocide. In *Genocide Studies International.* Maryland.

Fox, S. E. and Hartmut, B. 2002. A Neo-Aramaic dialect of Bohtan. In *„Sprich doch mit deinen Knechten aramäisch, wir verstehen es!" 60 Beiträge zur Semitistik.* Festschrift für Otto Jastrow zum 60. *Geburtstag,* edited by Werner A., 165-80. Wiesbaden.

Güner, M. 2011. *Turkisk-svensk, Svensk-turkisk ordbok.* Mölnlycke.

Greatrex, G. and Lieu, S. N. C. 2002. Roman frontier and foreign policy in the East. In *Justinian's First Persian War and the Eternal Peace.* London.

Hollerweger, H. 1999. *Turabdin - Living Cultural Heritage.* Linz.

Hopkins, S. 1989. Neo-Aramaic Dialects and the Formation of the Preterite. In *Journal of Semitic Studies* 34 (2): 413-432.

Jastrow, O. 1978. *Die Mesopotamisch-arabischen qəltu-Dialekte, I, Phonologie und Morphologie* (Abhandlungen für die Kunde des Morgenlandes, 43:4). Wiesbaden.

Jastrow, O. 1985. Mlaḥsō: An Unknown Neo-Aramaic Language of Turkey. In *Journal of Semitic Studies* 30, no. 2: 265-70.

Jastrow, O. 1987. The Ṭūrōyo language today. In *Journal of Assyrian Academic Studies* vol 1, 7-16.

Jastrow, O. 1988. *Der neuaramäische Dialekt von Hertevin (Provinz Siirt).* (Semitica Viva 3). Wiesbaden.

Jatrow, O. 1990. Personal and demonstrative pronouns in Central Neo-Aramaic. In *Studies in Neo-Aramaic,* edited by Heinrichs, B., 89-103. Atalanta.

Jastrow, O. 1993. *Laut und Formenlehre des neuaramḏischen Dialekts von Mīdin im Ṭūr ʿAbdin.* (Semitica Viva 9). Wiesbaden.

Jastrow, O. 1994. *Der neuaramäische Dialekt von Mlaḥsô.* (Semitica Viva 14). Wiesbaden.

Jastrow, O. and Shlomo, R. 1996. Passive formation in Turoyo and Melahso. In *Studies in Modern Semitic Languages,* edited by Shlomo I., 49-57. Leiden.

Jastrow, O. 1997. The Neo-Aramaic Languages. In *The Semitic Languages,* edited by Robert Hetzron, 334-377. London.

Jastrow, O. 2002 (first published 1992). *Lehrbuch der Ṭuroyo-Sprache.* (Semitica Viva 2). Wiesbaden.

Jastrow, O. 2005. Der bestimmte Artikel im Aramäishcen – ein Blick auf 3000 Jahre Sprachgeschichte. In *Studia Semitica et Semitohamitica. Festschrift für Rainer Voigt (Alter Orient und Altes Testament* 317*),* edited by Burta, B. et al., 137-150. Münster.

Khan, G. 1999. *A Grammar of Neo-Aramaic. The Dialect of the Jews of Arbel,* Handbook of Oriental Studies. Part 1: Ancient Near East 47. Leiden.

Lahdo, A. 2009. *The Arabic Dialect of Tillo in the Region of Siirt* (*South-eastern Turkey*). Uppsala.

Lahdo, A. 2014. Bequsyone, Texts reflecting cultural aspects in Tur Abdin. In *From Tur Abdin to Hadramawt.* Semitic Studies. Festschrift in Honour of Bo Isaksson on the occasion of his retirement. Wiesbaden.

Lahdo, A. 2013. The Martyrdom of Mōr ʿZuzoyo, A new Ṭūrōyo text from Kfarze in Ṭūr ʿAbdīn. In *Nicht nur mit Engelszungen.* Beiträge zur semitischen Dialektologie. Festschrift für Werner Arnold zum 60. Geburtstag. Wiesbaden.

Lewis, G. L. 2000. *Turkish Grammar.* Oxford.

Long, G. 1854. Amida. In William Smith, *Dictionary of Greek and Roman Geography,* Volume 1, Walton & Maberly.

Mutzafi, H. 2004. *The Jewish Neo-Aramaic dialect of Koy Sanjaq (Iraqi Kurdistan).* (Semitica Viva 32) Wiesbaden.

Nacim, J. 2003. *Turkarnas folkmord på assyrier-kaldéer och armenier.* Södertälje.

Ritter, H. 1967. *Ṭūrōyo: Die Volkssprache der syrischen Christen des Ṭūr ʕAbdīn. A, Texte, 1.* Beirut.

Ritter, H. 1969. *Ṭūrōyo: Die Volkssprache der syrischen Christen des Ṭūr ʕAbdīn. A, Texte, 2.* Beirut.

Ritter, H. and Orient-Institut der Deutschen morgenländischen Gesellschaft Beirut. 1971. *Ṭūrōyo: Die Volkssprache der syrischen Christen des Ṭūr ʕAbdīn. A, Texte, Bd 3*. Beirut.

Ritter, H. and Orient-Institut der Deutschen morgenländischen Gesellschaft Beirut. 1979. *Ṭūrōyo: Die Volkssprache der syrischen Christen des Ṭūr ʕAbdīn. B, Wörterbuch*. Beirut.

Ritter, H. and Rudolf S. 1990. *Ṭūrōyo: Die Volkssprache der syrischen Christen des Ṭūr ʕAbdīn. C, Grammatik: Pronomen, "sein, vorhanden sein", Zahlwort, Verbum.* Schriften der wissenschaftlichen Gesellschaft an der Johann Wolfgang Goethe-Universität Frankfurt/M. Geisteswissenschaftliche Reihe, 6. Stuttgart.

Sahbaz, Y. H. 2003. *Islams Vrede: en redogörelse om turkarnas massaker på kristna i Persien*. Södertälje.

Sinha, J. 2000. *Der neuostaramäische Dialekt von Bespen (Provinz Mardin, Südosttürkei). Eine grammatische Darstellung*. (Semitica viva 24). Wiesbaden.

Talay, S. 2002. Die aramäische Sprache (Turoyo) und ihre Zukunftsaussichten in der Diaspora. *The Journal of Eastern Christian Studies* 1-2: 65-76.

Talay, S. 2004. *Lebendig Begraben, Die Entführung des syrisch-orthodoxen Priesters Melki Tok von Midən in der Südosttürkei. Einführung, Aramäischer Text (Turoyo), Übersetzung und Glossar* (Studien zur Orientalischen Kirchengeschichte 29). Münster.

Talay, S. 2008. *Die Neuaramäischen Dialekte der Khabour-Assyrer in Nordostsyrien*. (Semitica Viva 40). Wiesbaden.

Talay, S. 2009. *Neuaramäische Texte in den Dialekten der Khabour-Assyrer in Nordostsyrien*. (Semitica Viva 41). Wiesbaden.

Tezel, A. 2003. *Comparative Etymological Studies in the Western Neo-Syriac (Ṭūrōyo) Lexicon. With Special Reference to Homonyms, Related Words and Borrowings with Cultural Signification. Uppsala.*

Tezel, S. 2011. *Arabic Borrowings in Ṣūrayt/Ṭūrōyo within the Framework of Phonological Correspondences. In Comparison with other Semitic Languages*. Uppsala.

Younansardaroud, H. 2001. *Der neuostaramäische Dialekt von Särdä:rïd*. (Semitica Viva 26). Wiesbaden.